Modern **C**ultu
——**T**heorists——

Roland Barthes

The following titles are available in the Modern Cultural Theorists Series:

Modern **C**ultural **T**heorists

Roland Barthes

Rick Rylance

**HARVESTER
WHEATSHEAF**

New York   London   Toronto   Sydney   Tokyo   Singapore

First published 1994 by
Harvester Wheatsheaf
Campus 400, Maylands Avenue
Hemel Hempstead
Hertfordshire, HP2 7EZ
A division of
Simon & Schuster International Group

Typeset in 11/12pt Ehrhardt
by Inforum, Rowlands Castle, Hants

Printed and bound in Great Britain by
Biddles Ltd, Guildford and King's Lynn

British Library Cataloguing in Publication Data

A catalogue record for this book is available from
the British Library

ISBN 0–7450–0721–X (hbk)
ISBN 0–7450–0722–8 (pbk)

1 2 3 4 5   98 97 96 95 94

For Ed Esche and Nigel Wheale

ideas in production

Contents

Author's preface

Roland Barthes's first two books form an interesting, contrasting pair. They are *Writing Degree Zero* (1953) and *Michelet* (1954), a book on the celebrated nineteenth-century historian. The first of these is abstract, general and theoretical; the second is playful, witty and textually specific. They thus establish the stylistic poles of Barthes's work. Here is the 'cold' Barthes of *Writing Degree Zero*, a sometimes demanding theorist who, as he later put it in his auto-biographical *Roland Barthes by Roland Barthes*, specialises in isolating 'the frozen word' (*RB*, 89). But here too is the 'hot' Barthes of *Michelet*. This Barthes is extravagant, impish and gamesome, delighting in the 'hot blood' of Michelet's turmoil and confusion, and it is this Barthes which he himself came to value most. Indeed, it is possible to track a development across Barthes's career using this polarity. Barthes's structuralism, his politics, and his preference for a modern aesthetics of austerity and colourlessness, belong to the cold order of the zero degree. As the first chapter will argue, this originates in his response to the exigencies of the Cold War and his pessimistic understanding of the modern individual's relationship to the general culture. The other, more carnivalesque Barthes, however, continues in disruptive dialogue with the pessimistic theorist. This Barthes enthusiastically enjoys the 'bourgeois' historian Michelet, relishes the cultural objects his politics ostensibly despise in *Mythologies*, and, in the closing part of his career, seeks *rapprochement* with its opposite in a series of intensely personal books.

It follows that I understand Barthes as an energetically dialectical writer somewhat in the spirit of similar figures from English letters like Keats or Lawrence. Like Barthes, these writers were hedonists in outlook. They stress the fine quality of individual response in a way which is difficult to reduce to summary argument. Barthes writes about Michelet, photography or fashion as Keats writes about art-works or Lawrence writes about the natural world. In reading them, something is learnt about these things, but the real centre of interest is the exchange between a writer's sensibility, a particular historical environment and a performance in language. Barthes's work, therefore, is not the professional criticism of the modern academy whose conventions he often defied. For Barthes, to respond to culture, even that of the past, was always to respond to the immediate. His work is therefore full of intensely contemporary dialectical engagements. In this it is like the kind of criticism written by Romantic essayists such as Hazlitt, or the great writer-critics Coleridge, Arnold or Eliot. Though from time to time Barthes tried to establish a 'method' (his structuralism is the best example) he often later regretted the restrictive stereotyping this involved. Our hindsight should follow his lead. In this book Barthes's work is understood as exploration, not as timeless methodology.

Finally, Barthes is an *international* writer. Though his tastes and some of his attitudes are insular (he remained pretty much a stranger to literatures other than French, for instance), his work has had spectacular international influence. This is for a number of reasons. It is because of the welcome increase in the international traffic of ideas. It is – in the English-speaking world, at least – because of the atrophy of native critical traditions by the time Barthes came to be translated in the late 1960s. Finally, it is because Barthes's ideas are not eccentric in the way both his supporters and opponents have sometimes made them appear. Though he assiduously cultivated his own individuality, Barthes speaks to concerns which have been at hand throughout this period in the West. One distinctive feature of this book, therefore, will be to examine the ways in which the ideas that interested Barthes have been integral not just to French culture, but also to debates within the English-speaking world. Barthes has travelled well because of his relevance to international concerns.

Acknowledgements

I would like to thank Peter Cattermole, Maud Ellmann and Nigel Wheale for reading this through, and for their many helpful suggestions. I would also like to thank Sam Hyde for tracking and chasing, Felicia Gordon and Simon Booy for various pieces of expert help, and Ian Gordon for general enabling, while at Harvester Jackie Jones has been wonderfully patient. But most of all I would like to thank Ann and David Booy in Cambridge, Sharon Ouditt and Martin Stannard in Leicester, and John Bailey and Meg Ousey in France for the friendship and hospitality which made this book writable while we were homeless. My thanks to my nomadic partner Judith Boddy is as great as ever because this book was written, and read by her, in no fewer than seven houses. Our thanks to Lol Sullivan for rebuilding the last of these is considerable.

Part of Chapter 3 first appeared in the essay 'Forms of dissent in contemporary drama and contemporary theory', in *The Death of the Playwright? Modern British drama and literary theory*, ed. Adrian Page (Macmillan, 1992).

Abbreviations and a note on words and texts

Roland Barthes has had the good fortune of excellent translators, and most of his work is now available in English. As I imagine that most readers will read more easily in English than in French, I refer to these translations throughout, adjusting them where I feel it is appropriate. I have used the following abbreviations in giving page references after each quotation. The particular editions used are listed in the Bibliography.

CE	*Critical Essays*
CL	*Camera Lucida*
Criticism	*Criticism and Truth*
Eiffel	*The Eiffel Tower and Other Mythologies*
Elements	*Elements of Semiology*
Empire	*Empire of Signs*
Fashion	*The Fashion System*
Grain	*The Grain of the Voice: Interviews 1962–1980*
IMT	*Image-Music-Text*
LD	*A Lover's Discourse*
Mich	*Michelet*
Myth	*Mythologies*
NCE	*New Critical Essays*
PoT	*The Pleasure of the Text*

Racine	*On Racine*
RB	*Roland Barthes by Roland Barthes*
Rustle	*The Rustle of Language*
SFL	*Sade/Fourier/Loyola*
Sollers	*Sollers Writer*
S/Z	*S/Z*
'Theory'	'Theory of the text'
WDZ	*Writing Degree Zero*

A note on the words 'Literature' and 'Text'

For reasons that will become clear in Chapter 1, the word *literature*, once uncontroversial, has become one of the most vexed terms in the contemporary critical lexicon. My own view is that much unfruitful fuss has been made about its definition, but readers need to be clear about the diversities of present usage. For some, the word represents a body of historically acquired writings with always-evident aesthetic value which are non-doctrinal and embody a triumphant human potential. For others, including the early Barthes, the term is much more ideologically contentious. For them, literature is an institution, not an aesthetic property. Its organisation follows the ideological orientation of those who organise it and, the world being as it is, this will be more or less in agreement with the status quo. I think both meanings are necessary. Literature is *both* an institutional event *and* a discursive resistance to it. But the two meanings must be separated. Accordingly, following Barthes's own practice, I will capitalise the word when it is used in the 'institutional' sense and accredit it to Barthes by quotation marks: 'Literature'.

Similarly, Barthes used the word *text* in a very particular sense to denote a desirable kind of avant-garde writing (see Chapter 3); but, of course, it has a more customary meaning. Barthes's version will therefore again be capitalised and strung between inverted commas: 'Text'.

Chronology

1915   12 November: Roland Barthes born in Cherbourg, son of Louis Barthes, a naval lieutenant, and Henriette Binger. Protestant on his mother's side, but Catholic on his father's – this is the first of the representative divisions Barthes detects in his life. He later describes his family background as solidly bourgeois.

1916   26 October: Louis Barthes killed in naval action in the North Sea, and posthumously decorated. Barthes's childhood is spent in the paternal family home at Bayonne, a coastal town in south-west France. Educated in local elementary school. A somewhat solitary period.

1924   Move to Paris, though Barthes continues to spend holidays in Bayonne and retains a lifelong attachment to the region. A period of some poverty. Mother earns a small living as a bookbinder. Beginnings of Barthes's education in the Parisian schools (a leading reason for moving to the capital).

1927   Birth of half-brother, Michel Salzado, out of wedlock. Relations with family strained. Barthes's

literary and political interests begin to be
established.

1933   Gains his *baccalauréat* in this and the following
            year; plans a novel, and writes his first text, a
            pastiche of Plato.

1934   Participates in the formation of DRAF, an anti-
            fascist political group. 10 May: first attack of
            pulmonary tuberculosis. October: sent to Bedous in
            the Pyrenees to recover. Increasing interest in the
            Classics, especially Greek, and an increasingly
            confident anti-Christian outlook.

1935–39   Sorbonne. French and Classics. Founder of the
            'Groupe de théâtre antique', with whom he travels
            to Greece and Italy. Exempted from military
            service but active in the Popular Front against
            fascism. Summer 1937: *Lecteur* in Hungary.

1939–40   Teacher in Biarritz (near Bayonne). June: Fall of
            Paris and Nazi Occupation.

1940–41   Teacher in Paris. Writing on Greek tragedy for
            Diplôme d'études supérieures (equivalent of MA).
            October 1941: tubercular relapse forces
            abandonment of the *agrégation*, the teaching
            examination.

1942   Sanatorium des étudiants, Saint-Hilaire-du-Touvet
            in the Isère, a liberal, intellectual enclave during the
            Occupation.

1943   Convalescence in Paris. Relapse in July.

1943–45   Return to Saint-Hilaire. Condition worsens.
            Barthes considers psychiatry as a career.

1945–46   Winter. Treatment at Swiss sanatorium at Leysin.
            Reading Michelet exhaustively. Developing interest
            in existentialism.

1946–47   Convalescence in Paris. Begins to move in postwar
            Parisian literary circles and plans work on Michelet,
            Camus, Greek theatre and (anticipating *A Lover's*

Discourse) a 'book on love'. Writes for Camus's journal *Combat*. These pieces later incorporated in *Writing Degree Zero*.

1947–49   Unable to find work in Paris, accepts job as librarian, then teacher, at L'Institut français in Bucharest. Growing interest in popular culture, especially music. All institute staff expelled in July 1949 by hard-line Romanian government. Sartre, *What is Literature?*

1949–50   Reader at University of Alexandria in Egypt. Introduced to advanced modern linguistics by A.J. Greimas, also a lecturer at the university. Barthes's first exposure to colonial attitudes, which he detests. Continues to write for prominent left-wing periodicals.

1950–52   Works in the education department of the Direction générale des relations culturelles, Paris.

1952–54   Lexicographer at CNRS (Centre national de la recherche scientifique). Increasing interest in linguistics. Co-founder of radical journal *Théâtre populaire*. Polemicising for Robbe-Grillet and Brecht after publication of the former's *Les Gommes* in 1953 and the visit to Paris of Brecht's Berliner Ensemble in 1954.

1953   Begins regular 'Mythologies' columns for *Les lettres nouvelles*. *Writing Degree Zero* published by new radical publisher Seuil. Substantial personal inheritance after death of grandmother. Poujade's 'Union de défense de commerçants et artisans' founded (first electoral success in 1956).

1954   *Michelet*. Beginning of Algerian War (lasts until 1962) and French withdrawals in SE Asia.

1955   Transfers to sociology section of CNRS (until 1959). Involved in polemical controversy with Camus. Friendship with Foucault begins.

1957   *Mythologies*.

attitude is distantly supportive. His radical heyday is over. Begins the auto-critique of structuralism in his still-popular seminar. Sollers, *Writing and the Experience of Limits*.

1969–70   In Morocco. Lectures at the University of Rabat.

1970   *S/Z; Empire of Signs*.

1971   *Sade/Fourier/Loyola*; 'From work to text'.

1972   *New Critical Essays*. Deleuze and Guattari, *Anti-Oedipus*.

1973   *The Pleasure of the Text*.

1974   Trip to China with Sollers, Kristeva and others.

1975   *Roland Barthes by Roland Barthes*.

1976   Barthes elected to a Chair in Literary Semiology at the Collège de France, France's most prestigious academic institution.

1977   *A Lover's Discourse*; inaugural lecture at the Collège de France (published in 1978 as *Leçon*). 'Prétexte: Roland Barthes': colloquium on Barthes's work at Cerisy-la-Salle. 25 October: death of mother. Barthes becomes increasingly depressed.

1979   *Sollers Writer*.

1980   *Camera Lucida*. 25 February: injured in a traffic accident near the Collège de France. 26 March: Barthes dies in hospital.

Historical and cultural context

Historically, Barthes lived through a number of key developments in the postwar world, and his work was profoundly influenced by them. In France, there was the trauma of the Nazi Occupation during World War II and the exigencies of the postwar recovery. Because of his illness, Barthes spent the war years in sanatoria, so he came late to these conditions. But he was a youthful supporter of the Popular Front against fascism, and read enthusiastically in existentialist writing, the most prestigious intellectual movement of the day, which owed its kudos in part to the role played by some of its most prominent figures, especially Sartre, in the Resistance. The existentialists were opponents of mainstream culture. They believed that human beings should define their 'authenticity' uniquely as individuals, and not accept the hand-me-down roles offered to them by society. People who failed to live their lives with full commitment and awareness lived in 'bad faith', and existentialist fiction dramatised the collision between individuals trying to live in this way and the prevailing cultural ethos. Meanwhile, as we shall see in Chapter 1, Sartre urged writers to commit themselves deliberately to social causes. The writer was to be a self-defining individual, but with unavoidable social responsibilities.

Barthes accepted the existential definition of the relationship between the individual and the general culture. He too saw society imposing its inauthentic norms on individuals. But he could not accept the more optimistic commitments in Sartre's thinking. For him, the individual and society are permanently at odds, and this is probably the most persistent dynamic in his work. Despite Sartre's prestige, French culture in the 1950s was effectively refurbishing its old structures, and was fundamentally antipathetic to the values of the dissident Left. Barthes's work, therefore, begins in dissent, but with a pessimism which was a product of both temperament and circumstance. Specifically, as I shall argue in more detail in Chapter 1, his work takes shape in the psychological conditions of the Cold War and the feeling of being trapped in a global situation which Europeans were powerless to change. Barthes writes of this specifically in *Mythologies*, but it also forms the background to his most celebrated methodological innovation, structuralism (see Chapter 2). Structuralism stresses the power of the governing structure at the expense of the freedom of the individual. It thus shares the Cold War sense of individual powerlessness, and underlines the pessimism in Barthes's early existentialism.

Barthes's work in the late 1950s and early 1960s tackles other issues which relate closely to developments in other parts of Europe. The increasingly vigorous presence of an American-influenced, commercialised popular culture, and the resulting concern about the decline of traditional values and the current role of education and literature, were everywhere debated with different emphases. But perhaps the most important issue was the large-scale imperial withdrawal by the European powers. Having worked in Egypt in the late 1940s, Barthes was especially concerned about North Africa, where France had substantial territories (particularly in Algeria, where a deadly war of independence was being fought at the end of the 1950s). Difficulties abroad provoked crisis at home, in particular the collapse of the constitution and the foundation of de Gaulle's Fifth Republic in 1958. In addition, there was a revival of the reactionary Right under its populist leader Pierre Poujade, mentor to Jean-Marie Le Pen, the current leader of the racist Front National. Barthes attacked Poujadism in *Mythologies* (*Eiffel*, 51–4, 127–36) for its militant anti-intellectualism which took the tone of a general culture he perceived as aggressively complacent and increasingly politically managed. This general climate was assailed in *Mythologies*, and other structuralist work describes an arid consumer wasteland mirroring similar anxieties across the West (see Chapter 2). His alignment with the intellectual avant-garde originates in a period when, for the only time in his life, he seriously contemplated leaving France.[1]

In his poststructuralist phase, Barthes's work became increasingly radical, though his politics were more a matter of general dissidence than a settled position. Like several in his circle he flirted with Maoism in the early 1970s, but became increasingly individualistic in outlook. He takes it for granted that mainstream culture stifles individuals, a view common among dissident intellectuals in the late 1960s. In response, Barthes became more and more absorbed in the disruptive, playful energies of avant-garde literary language as a model for the best style of living. These ideas reflect the political events of the near-revolution of 1968, towards which Barthes's feelings were, however, ambivalent. As a result, he was forced to redefine the avant-garde and revalue traditional cultural works against 'countercultural' incitements. The resulting paradox – an iconoclastic guardian of traditional culture – is at the hub of much of his last work which, somewhat contrary to his earlier anti-humanism, re-examines personal issues with a growing sensitivity to intimate, individual experience.

The critical reputation of Barthes's work is easy to characterise. He pictured himself, and was pictured by opponents and supporters alike, as a critical radical and leading spokesman for the 'Nouvelle Critique' which has transformed critical and cultural thinking in the West over the past three decades. He has been a part of every major intellectual movement in the humanities that has come out of France since the war, and his international standing is secure. Part of Barthes's success has come about because the structuralism and poststructuralism of his intellectual generation have spoken so powerfully to the needs and circumstances of Anglo-American criticism. By the mid-1960s, the mainstream literary theory established in the early decades of this century in Britain and America had ceased to command assent, and Barthes's work overturns several central principles of it.

Where traditional Anglo-American criticism despised popular culture, Barthes seemed to revel in it; where the older criticism revered tradition, Barthes flaunted his topicality; where the older work was intellectually cautious, the new was searchingly adventurous; where the old was politically conservative, Barthes seemed ostentatiously radical; where the old cherished the virtues of formal balance and the simple, rural life, Barthes relished the urban sophistication of the avant-garde and the fragmentary. Barthes championed new writing and appeared more in step with contemporary work, while his own flamboyant style – though it has since been wearisomely imitated – ostentatiously defamiliarised the clichés of the older criticism. The 'Nouvelle Critique' seemed modern and 'relevant', and carried the prestige of exciting new methods and approaches. Finally, it became increasingly clear that this new thinking was in tune with the revolution in electronic communications which has radically altered the infrastructure of modern cultural production (see Chapter 3). Barthes perceived this early in an essay for *Mythologies* entitled 'The two salons' (*Eiffel*, 137–40), and his prescience has been corroborated.

In retrospect, it is doubtful whether Barthes's work sustains all of these claims. His attitudes to, for instance, popular culture or radical politics now seem much more ambiguous, and it is certainly true that if his work is companionable with the new technologies, he also cultivated the image of an amateur man of letters in a distinctly old-fashioned sense. In this way and others, the Barthesian hybrid of new and old can be seen as part of the phenomenon of postmodern cultural theory.

But this book tries to set Barthes in a cultural context beyond the polarities both he and his opponents invited. In an early interview he speaks of the need for a 'parallel – and relational – history' of modern culture (*CE*, 265). He had in mind the need to relate 'the popular' and 'the literary', but the phrase is applicable in a different sense. This account of Barthes will look steadily at parallel and relational developments in the Anglo-American world which form a significant part of the wider historical and cultural context of his work.

<table>
<tr><td>CHAPTER
ONE</td><td>Barthes hot and cold:
early work</td></tr>
</table>

Judging by nausea

As is the case with many writers, Barthes's early work is not easily classifiable in the terms by which he later became best known. None the less, his first two books illustrate the two poles of his analytic imagination, and begin themes which preoccupied him throughout his career. This chapter will therefore raise issues which will be reconsidered as the account of his work develops. The first section will examine *Michelet*; the second *Writing Degree Zero*. The third will broaden the scope to look at Barthes's confrontation with French academic orthodoxy in the celebrated 'Picard affair' of the early 1960s.

Throughout this period Barthes is on the radical wing of French intellectual opinion, and his work combatively assimilates new thinking from psychoanalysis, phenomenology, and the radical aesthetics of Brechtian drama and the 'nouveau roman' (all of which will be considered as we proceed). This loose and, by later standards, not very shapely ensemble is held together by an axiomatic Leftist politics (the limits of which we will explore in Chapter 2), and a careful response to Sartre's existential Marxism, the dominant intellectual current of the period in dissident circles. Barthes began with existentialism, and in a sense he ended with it,

1

for his final book is a homage to Sartre's *L'Imaginaire*. This chapter will therefore situate Barthes's existentialism, although it is difficult to label the early period 'existentialist' in the way we may call later phases 'structuralist' or 'poststructuralist'. His early work has neither the same methodological rigour nor the sustained commitment of these later developments. Instead we see a writer exploring a territory, exuberant and bleak by turns, but always powerfully at odds with orthodoxy.

Writing Degree Zero was Barthes's first book, but not his first piece of research. A sufferer from tuberculosis, he spent much of his early life, including the war years, in sanatoria. Already a promising scholar, he was sent to clinics with good libraries, and in one of these, with time on his hands, Barthes began his lifelong enthusiasm for the nineteenth-century historian Jules Michelet, author of two dozen books and a twenty-volume history of France. He began in what became his habitual research method: reading slowly, gathering his information on 'fiches', index cards, in the method taught in French schools.[1] This was – unwittingly – admirably suited to his subsequent practice: it avoids integrative narrative and argumentative continuity, it dismantles a work into fragments, and it looks forward to the new information age ('fiches' were an early way of loading computers). Barthes's early methods forecast his career.

His book on Michelet, *Michelet par lui-même*, was published in 1954 in a well-known series of introductory books on celebrated writers, 'Écrivains de toujours'. The aim of the series is to introduce the subject by way of substantial extracts with commentary. The proper academic apparatus is provided – chronological outline, guide to further reading – and the texts have a nice illustrated finish. Yet Barthes's *Michelet* at once appears odd: the chapter titles are disconcerting – 'Michelet, eater of history', 'History, which we so stupidly decline in the feminine', 'The Ultra-Sex', and so on – and his conventional 'Memorandum' of details is brusque to the point of irony: 'ANCESTRY: . . . The Millets of Renwez (Ardennes). A very pious mother' (*Mich*, 5). Barthes also begins by telling his readers what they will not find: a précis of Michelet's life and thought, or an explanation of the one by the other. Instead, he wishes 'to recover the structure of an existence (if not a life), a thematics, if you like, or better still: an organised network of obsessions' (*Mich*, 3). Already, several central Barthesian themes are gathered: a prickly syntax and tone which challenges and redefines, a startling casting of a canonical writer as a structure of psychological obsessions, a promise of a quasi-technical method ('thematics'), and an aggressive existential framework which not only declares a dismissive attitude towards the small change of conventional criticism, but also flaunts his alignment with the radical existentialism of the day.

Michelet, like much of Barthes, sets out to shock. Its lengthy account of Michelet's sexuality, for instance, was flamboyantly provoking in a period before the publication of the historian's celebrated intimate journal, and the 'Écrivains de toujours' series provided a fine opportunity for a young iconoclast. There is a strong convention – the introductory textbook – to kick against, and Michelet's reputation prompts a game with critical authority. Meanwhile, the extract-and-commentary format allows Barthes to dramatise the play between text and critical discourse, which he emphasises by printing the two in different typefaces, an innovation for the series. This, and the illustrations, enable him to break up the surface of his book in ways that he used more extravagantly as his career developed. But *Michelet*'s main concern is a theme which was topical in the Sartrean environment of postwar Paris, and became an abiding preoccupation for Barthes throughout his career: the question of how much freedom Michelet had as a writer. Barthes does not have in mind the empirical constraints of research or publication. His concern is with the more or less unconscious forces which shape Michelet's writing, because for Barthes all writing is written under powerful personal and ideological pressures which shape it almost independently of conscious choice. Existentially, a writer should, of course, resist these pressures of convention and ideology, which wreck the authenticity of a work. But in the case of a historian like Michelet, Barthes is interested in the ways in which historical events are none the less moulded to express what he calls the writer's 'themes': those consistent patterns which are the bare bones of his 'existence'.

Barthes defines a 'theme' as 'a critical reality independent of the idea, and of the image' (*Mich*, 201). That is, it is an ingredient of the text which shapes it in a way that is almost separate from the explicit meaning or intention. It is a kind of elemental feature, a mixture of style and personal obsession, which organises the discourse's flow. Themes can be recognised because they are repeated, and Michelet's include his ideological position (starkly presented in the 'Memorandum' as the 'classic credo of the liberal petit-bourgeois around 1840', *Mich*, 11) and his methodological preferences as a historian. But Barthes's special concern is the unconscious psychology of the writing: the way an obsessional interest in a series of substances, properties or processes organises Michelet's narratives, and therefore shapes the reader's understanding. Nations, events or persons have for him a quasi-allegorical significance, and exemplify the grand rhythms which run throughout all history. England, for example, is described in terms of angularity or hardness; Germany is fragmentary; but France is smooth and seamless, like the blend of ingredients in a recipe (*Mich*, 27–30). The historical 'facts' do not matter: it is their rhetorical organisation which is significant for Barthes, who detects consistent patterns. When Michelet describes something positively, he reaches for images of blood, viscosity or warmth. When he is being negative, the language emphasises hardness, dryness or blockage.

At a personal level, and more controversially, Barthes argues that Michelet's writing plays out his sexual obsessions. His descriptions of historical processes are constructed according to deep psychosexual wishes, and Barthes's selections illustrate how, for instance, Michelet contradictorily juxtaposes idealised visions of the family (an ideological value) with a rampant voyeurism in his physical descriptions of historical 'characters': 'Ripe, pious, sugary, still fresh, plump and lovely', writes Michelet of the extraordinarily oxymoronic body of Louis XV's seducer, the Comtesse de Toulouse (*Mich*, 93). On a larger scale, Barthes suggests that Michelet's version of the historical process is modelled on a bizarre, diagrammatic sexuality in which Man represents the Idea, and Woman is Instinct. These roles are filled by different agents in different periods, but their procreation brings about the historical event. Michelet's historiography, therefore, is an endless retelling of this same story with a different cast list. As a form of explanation it is, to say the least, dubious, and indulges a fairly typical piece of nineteenth-century gender-typing. But Barthes's point is that Michelet is inexplicit about these narratives. They form an unconscious thematic pattern which is assumed in the writing but none the less constructs the reader's understanding of the world; and this, Barthes argues, is characteristic of all forms of representational writing. What Michelet's writing does so spectacularly is what all such writing does – even historiography, which claims to represent things as they really happened: it provides an interpretation of the world in which details are mere illustration. Barthes's thinking along these lines responds directly to innovative ways of thinking in postwar historiography, literary criticism and philosophy.

Barthes had worked briefly in this period with the celebrated 'Annales' school, which was then overturning French thinking about historical method and the relationship between the written version and actual events.[2] Like the slightly later 'history from below' associated with E.P. Thompson, Christopher Hill, Rodney Hilton and others in Britain, the 'Annales' school (named after their journal) tried to present history as the structure of everyday life. 'Annales' history was, therefore, critical of prevailing versions of history, and constructed alternatives. Barthes's work can be seen in a similar way. His book dismantles the historiographical principles on which Michelet's work is built by finding within them an alternative dynamic. The whole spread of the work is thus reassembled on thematic rather than chronological lines, and Michelet's writing is seen to be organised by non-referential elements rather than communicating the 'truth' of the past. As we shall see, this idea is crucial for Barthes. For him writing does not convey 'reality' as such, it organises constructions of it; thus the metaphors writers use represent the most forceful dynamic of their work. Later, Barthes found support for this view in Nietzsche, but it is a pervasive early argument, and his own metaphorical extravagance (ideal domesticity is like a canal boat, Michelet eats history and aspires to be a lesbian, no less) tries rhetorically to combat it by making the effect spectacular. In terms of literature, this is the beginning of Barthes's anti-realist aesthetics.

In a sense, *Michelet* applies the methods of literary criticism to history. This procedure has been adopted subsequently in a more thoroughgoing way by historiographical radicals like Hayden White, who argues that even modern work remains dependent on its rhetorical organisation.[3] From a literary point of view, the critical method most prominently used in *Michelet* is that of the 'phenomenological' school associated then in France with critics like Georges Poulet, Jean Starobinski and Jean-Pierre Richard.[4] Phenomenologists argue that objects cannot be considered independently of the consciousness which perceives them, and phenomenological criticism is interested in how writing expresses the particular ways in which a writer constructs the world, or how it organises a reader's perceptions. Object and consciousness are two sides of the same coin. Literary works, therefore, are not thought of as always having the same meaning, because meaning will vary depending on the consciousness which constructs it. Nor are they able 'objectively' to convey reality. In Barthes's view, for example, Michelet constructs history through his obsessional themes, and Barthes's role as a critic is to reveal the patterning.

Barthes's approach is a radical blend of phenomenology and psychoanalysis, but an illuminating comparison can be made with equivalent, but more moderate, projects in Anglo-American criticism, which has also sometimes been influenced by a version of phenomenology. Both J. Hillis Miller's *Charles Dickens: The world of his novels* (1958), which is dedicated to Georges Poulet, and John Carey's *The Violent Effigy* (1973) provide points of comparison with Barthes's work in *Michelet*. Both are about Dickens, whose driven and chaotic nineteenth-century imagination is – interestingly – not unlike that of Michelet. All three books set themselves to discover the 'unity' of their subject's imagination: 'the original unity of a creative mind', as Miller puts it, which imposes an 'impalpable organizing form, constantly presiding over the choice of words'.[5] Similarly, Carey, who likens Dickens's imagination to that of archetypal modernists like Sartre and Kafka who influenced Barthes, aims to recover the structure of Dickens's 'mode of thought', his 'imaginative world' independent of theories about his 'inner life' or his work's 'inner meanings'.[6] What follows in these books is an exploration of the often grotesque shape Dickens gives to a world in which phenomena, like historical events in Michelet, are a function of the verbal imagination which displays them.

Like Barthes, both critics see a radical separation between the world in writing and the world as it is in actuality. It is here, however, that Barthes parts company. For Miller, Dickens's imagination transcends this separation to provide a different 'truth'. The novels 'transform the real world of Dickens's experience into an imaginary world with certain special qualities of its own', he argues (Miller, 328). The 'real world' for Dickens is one of radical alienation, but his fiction offers 'something transcendent, something more than one's own consciousness or than the too solid everyday material world' (Miller, 329). In Miller's view this is the discovery of 'a real self' which lies beyond the everyday self, and is above the latter's ordinary pressures and limitations. Similarly for Carey, who is less ambitious, the novels create a drama in which Dickens's corrosive comedy and 'amoral and unprincipled' imagination are transformed and controlled (Carey, 9, 175). In both cases what starts out as disorder or alienation is converted into its opposite.

Barthes's book, by contrast, stresses the untransformable outrageousness of Michelet's imagination. Miller and Carey are primarily interested in Dickens's *art* which – for Miller, at least – explicitly needs to transcend the social world to become authentic. In this Miller follows the tradition of analysis set out by American New Criticism, which generally celebrates literary creativity in these terms. For Barthes, on the other hand, Michelet's writing flaunts its contradictions, and Barthes is not interested in finding meanings (Miller's 'real self') or effects (the emollient power of comedy in Carey) to transcend this instability. What is primarily of interest to him is the manic scribbling which Michelet's hapless predicament produces. If Barthes is suspicious of Michelet's ideology, he revels in a writing which comes from the historian's desperate attempt to make the world, the self and language cohere after all. Barthes quotes Michelet to the effect that he wanted to find an unalienated language which might speak directly for 'the People', and remarks that 'based on the alliance of the two sexes, the People gradually becomes in Michelet a superior means of knowledge'. What Michelet really desires is 'the abolition of all contraries, the magical restoration of a seamless world which is no longer torn between contradictory postulations' (*Mich*, 187). In other words, Michelet strives to efface the problems his own writing presents, and to pass it off as a neutral medium through which events speak directly. In this he 'is perhaps the first writer of modernity able to utter only an impossible language' (*Mich*, 188).

As a number of commentators observe, Barthes's Michelet is actually a portrait of the existential intellectual of the 1950s, a writer 'of modernity' struggling, in Sartrean fashion, to establish a bond with the collective voice which will overcome his alienation. Barthes's existentialism will be discussed more fully in the next section, but in *Michelet* it is both emphatic and problematic. He comments that for Michelet 'the human body is entirely an immediate judgement, but its value is of an existential not an intellectual order. Michelet condemns by virtue of his nauseas, not of his principles' (*Mich*, 92). Barthes sees Michelet's 'morality of the body', his 'tribunal of the flesh' (*Mich*, 203), as an inevitable existential and writerly condition. Whatever Michelet wills, his psychology, his historical situation and the nature of language itself force him back to his corporeal and 'thematic' preoccupations. Michelet's involuntary judgemental 'nausea' (a carefully chosen Sartrean image) is heavily determined, and Michelet seems doomed to repeat his extravagances without limit. Existentially, therefore, Barthes's view is pessimistic. The positive will seems a second-order psychological power, and Michelet appears unable to become an agent in the destiny of his own writing. Here Barthes opposes the transcendent view of art which was typical of both the Anglo-American and French critical mainstream in the period.

But Barthes enjoys his Michelet thoroughly. What he takes pleasure in is the bizarre edge to the writing, and he portrays the quixotic historian as heroic in his helplessness, authentic within his inauthenticity. As with several figures in his later work – such as the lover or the man in mourning – Barthes understands Michelet's predicament with a sometimes unflattering comic sympathy, while he reads him against himself. He relishes the creativity which sprawls across his unalterable predicament, but treats with severe scepticism his claims to truth or knowledge. This playful absorption in the density of writing and phenomena is the 'hot' Barthes which is one pole of his work. In the next section we shall see the other: the more analytic Barthes, resisting Sartre's optimism and finding that the only cure for nausea is a chilly dose of the zero degree.

Solitary style

Writing Degree Zero is a very different book from *Michelet*. Where *Michelet* has a Rabelaisian relish for the body and the grotesque, *Writing Degree Zero* is austere and, in the high Parisian manner, cultivates a cool remoteness of tone and argument. This style, however, is not inappropriate to the book's theme. *Writing Degree Zero* is preoccupied with the problem of how original writing can be undertaken in a stiflingly conventional world. Its abstemious style reflects its case for a deliberate disengagement from a damaging ordinariness. The book's radical argument is therefore one of disengagement, and its Leftist politics are those of the solitary. As such, *Writing Degree Zero* addresses significant general issues in postwar culture, and relates closely to companion developments in Britain in the same period. It also marks Barthes's most significant disagreement with Sartre.

The first page of *Writing Degree Zero* poses the crucial existential question of the 'stand we take' in history (*WDZ*, 1). In *Michelet*, Barthes, in a sense, exonerates the helpless obedience of Michelet's pen from accusations of bad faith by revelling in the writing it produces. But in *Writing Degree Zero* the question of the individual's relationship to the dominant discourse, and his responsibility to resist it, is put much more starkly as a choice of 'moral attitude' to language (*WDZ*, 2). The dominant influence in this argument is Sartre, whose *What is Literature?* (1948) posed the central question for the postwar generation who had come through the Nazi Occupation: how is literature situated in relation to the dominant culture? Is it in the service of freedom or not? For Sartre, and for Barthes following him, personal situations have inescapable public dimensions. *Writing Degree Zero*, therefore, starts on a different tack from *Michelet*, and Barthes is primarily interested in the social, not the psychological. But in addressing this question, he begins to diverge radically from Sartre, his existential mentor.

The argument of *Writing Degree Zero* is relatively easy to summarise. For Barthes, as for the Russian Formalists before him, literature is essentially an activity of language, and it is the use of appropriate formal language that makes a work literary. But this formal language is powerfully underwritten by conventions, approved vocabularies, standards of 'taste', ranges of reference, and so forth, which shape its acceptable 'readability' in any period. Therefore, to be 'Literature' (and henceforth Barthes's meaning will be indicated in this way), writing needs to conform to prevailing standards of expression. 'Literature', therefore, is fundamentally an *institutional* use of language, and here lies the major difference between Barthes and the Russian Formalists. For the latter, literature happens when writers *resist* the norm and 'defamiliarise' conventions. The essential dynamic is one of innovation and estrangement. For Barthes, on the other hand, the essential dynamic is one of incorporation. To thrive, authors need to advertise their literariness; their work must display the signs of 'Literature' which prevail in their period. Barthes compares the process to a baptism.

Barthes, therefore, wants a new literary history – not of the works of the great, but of the very 'signs of Literature' which give it institutional identity. He has in mind the study of stylistic rules, the evolution of generic conventions, or the more nebulous area of 'taste'. Following Sartre's lead in *What is Literature?*, Barthes provides a polemical sketch of French literary development, concentrating particularly on the establishment of 'bourgeois' writing in the nineteenth century and its extension to the present. It is a highly schematic outline of the ways in which language is institutionally shackled:

> Born in the seventeenth century in the group that was closest to the people, shaped by the force of dogmatic decisions, promptly ridding itself of all grammatical turns of speech forged by the spontaneous subjectivity of ordinary people, and drilled, on the contrary, for a task of definition, bourgeois writing was first presented, with the cynicism customary in the first flush of political victory, as the language of the privileged minority. (*WDZ*, 57–8)

In its multiplication of clauses, each beginning with a powerful verb, the language mimics the accretive atrophy of literary language. It is an un-nuanced, unempirical style which became established as the dominant mode of discourse on the European Left. (It was imported into Britain by the *New Left Review* in the late 1960s). It is a language which totalises structures and processes, and in *Writing Degree Zero* even dissident work is dragged into the neutralising machinery of 'Literature'. The 'naturalism' of Zola or Maupassant is a case in point.

Originally a protest writing, Naturalism aimed to reveal conditions among, for example, miners in Northern France or the Parisian underclass to a conventional literary readership. But the inevitable division between the subject matter and the readership, Barthes argues, betrays these ambitions because Zola is forced to turn his material into 'Literature'. This contaminates the intention, because the content lies outside the approved forms of 'Literature' in a 'period when bourgeois ideology conquered and triumphed' (*WDZ*, 56). Naturalism's 'technicization of writing' –

the effort to describe the world with the chilly horror of an autopsy
– shocks initially but ends up 'more artificial' than the language it
aims to supplant (*WDZ*, 67). Furthermore, the new language is
then itself incorporated as a standard for 'Literature' which is all
the more insidious because Naturalism, still pretending not to be
'Literature', simply suppresses its literariness on the grounds of
realism. It is then transmitted through the education system:

> Between a proletariat excluded from all culture, and an intel-
> ligentsia which had already begun to question Literature itself, the
> average public produced by primary and secondary schools, namely
> lower-middle-class, roughly speaking, will therefore find in this
> artistic-realistic mode of writing – which is that of a good propor-
> tion of commercial novels – the image *par excellence* of a Literature
> which has all the striking and intelligible signs of its identity. In
> this case the function of the writer is not so much to create a work
> as to supply a Literature which can be seen from afar. (*WDZ*, 69–
> 70)

Like something from a Cold War science-fiction movie, 'Literature' is a creature that thrives on the antidote designed to kill it.
Naturalism's worthy protest is snatched away, and the 'artistic-
realistic mode of writing' is transmitted to the next generation as
the very sign of 'Literature' itself. There are clear overlaps here
with the argument of *Michelet*.

Barthes's objection to realism in *Writing Degree Zero* is part
ethical, part political. Realism is unethical because it acts in existential bad faith by failing to declare its fabricatedness. It pretends
to represent the world faithfully, but only by suppressing the signs
of its own literariness. And realism is a problem politically because
this duplicity eventually serves ruling interests, as 'Literature' is
inevitably identified with the status quo. It 'is when history is
denied', Barthes writes, 'that it is most unmistakably at work'
(*WDZ*, 2). *Writing Degree Zero* is therefore an agitatory book which
relentlessly conflates the literary and the political. It can also be a
depressing book. Its historical schema is obdurate and polemical,
and severely limits the claim by Sartrean existentialists that writers
can choose to be free. It replicates on a social and historical level
the argument made by *Michelet* at a psychological level, and as
such it is very much of its period. As history, it is thin on detail,
but as an account of a significant strand of postwar literary culture

it makes fascinating sense. It defines a modern 'problematics of language' in relation to a role for artists and intellectuals which has telling resonances among other Cold War experiences. Its portrait of literary culture as increasingly homogenised, and artists and intellectuals as increasingly isolated, is very familiar, as is the argument that traditional forms no longer bond new work to the cultural mainstream.

I am thinking here of writers like Doris Lessing and Sylvia Plath in Britain. Lessing, for instance, in 'A small personal voice', an essay written for Tom Maschler's *Declaration* volume in 1957, attacked contemporary British writing for its complacency and insularity.[7] Like Barthes, she portrayed the dominant culture as narrow and incorporative, and the formal properties of its literature as incapable of registering the significantly new. Also like Barthes she looked back to the nineteenth century. Unlike Barthes, however, she found there not the bourgeois confiscation of literature in the duplicities of realism, but an opposite estimation. For Lessing, nineteenth-century realism offered a model for the contemporary novel which might break the ingrown triviality of British writing, and provide a valuable integration of personal and social experience. Lessing was not alone in this opinion. The same themes can be found in Raymond Williams's chapter on the contemporary novel in *The Long Revolution* (1961), and it illustrates a significant difference between some English and French attitudes to realism amongst oppositional intellectuals. But what is interesting about Lessing's use of nineteenth-century realism is, first, that against the conservative national-canonical evaluation of it by Leavisite critics (*The Great Tradition* had appeared only eight years previously), realism for Lessing is an international tradition straddling Europe from Middlemarch to Moscow. Hence her charge of insularity against contemporary British work.

But the second and more important point is that when, in *The Golden Notebook* (1962), Lessing came to write a modern version of the form, it fell apart in her hands as dramatically as the psychology of its central character. The novel does not sustain the claim that realism provides a valuable 'balance' of the social, psychological, political and personal which her 1971 Preface continued to make. Instead, Lessing uses the implosion of the form to enact the instabilities of the period. The novel divides into compartmentalised notebooks, and the 'truth' of the action is unreachably distributed between the parallel segments, while the language is increasingly disrupted by parody, fragmentation, disturbed personal report and a lurid newspaper-speak which announce the chilling emergencies of decolonisation, the Cold War and the testing of the H-bombs. The imagery derived from these events – icy cold, ominous clouds, scraps of frighteningly incomplete information – increasingly infiltrates the description of psychological collapse. The sense of breakdown and entrapment *The Golden Notebook* portrays is, in its 'structure of feeling' (Raymond Williams's celebrated concept was itself coined in 1961), strikingly similar to that outlined in *Writing Degree Zero* and described in less abstract mood in the essay 'Martians' from *Mythologies* (1957). Here Barthes addresses the Cold War nuclear stalemate directly as a global 'psychosis' for which the popular interest in invasions from outer space is a displacement. His description has the same appalled clarity as that experienced by the equally alienated protagonist of Lessing's novel:

> it postulates the existence of a Super-Nature from the sky, for it is in the sky that the Terror exists: the sky is henceforth without metaphor, the field where atomic death appears. The judge is born in the same site where the executioner threatens. (*Eiffel*, 29)

Nature is no Romantic metaphor. The sky itself, Providence, 'a Super-Nature', represents a retributive menace because the 'great USSR/USA standoff is henceforth perceived as a guilty state, since the danger is out of proportion to any justification' (*Eiffel*, 27). It is a reversion to an epoch of superstition.

The Cold War 'psychosis' and the parallel disintegration of realistic 'balance' in Lessing's work establishes, but also adjusts, Barthes's argument, because the position taken in *Writing Degree Zero* is rather formalistic. For all its emphasis on history, *Writing Degree Zero* confines discussion to the formal properties of literary language, with little regard for content. *The Golden Notebook*, by contrast, is fully enmeshed in the messy detail of the period, and the fact that it is *specifically* about the H-bomb, South Africa, Cuba, and so on is crucial. But *The Golden Notebook* also confirms Barthes's argument that new writing is made from the collapse of accepted languages. Its central character is a novelist, Anna Wulf, who has a writer's block; that is, her experience and her language are no longer co-ordinated. In *Writing Degree Zero* Barthes also describes the situation of the writer as a blockage, and suggests that 'every man is a prisoner of his language'. Writing is a 'blind alley . . . because society itself is a blind alley' (*WDZ*, 87). These images of imprisonment, blindness, alienation, paralysis and blockage are of a piece in both works. Like Anna Wulf, Barthes's writer is inevitably solitary (*WDZ*, 4) and disjoined: there is a 'tragic disparity between what he [the writer] does and what he sees' (*WDZ*, 86).

If the leading argument of *Writing Degree Zero* concerns blockage and inhibition, however, the book is also about creativity, and in particular how, in this existentially bleak scenario, the writer might find a fleeting freedom by resistance to incorporative language. Once again, Barthes is closer to a general mood than is sometimes thought. Intellectuals in *The Golden Notebook* find haven in neither tradition nor dissent, and this isolation preoccupies many writers whose work couples a stark diagnostic clarity to a sustained ambiguity about purposes. Beckett is exemplary in this respect, but much writing of the period dramatises a defeating encounter with a cultural orthodoxy which in Britain is usually called 'Tradition', and Barthes called 'Literature'.

This is observable in Sylvia Plath's poetry, for example, of whose innovative formal and verbal energies Barthes would perhaps have approved. 'The Colossus' (1959) is a case in point.[8] It is a poem about a shattered male icon, a broken and inert emblem of cultural tradition over which the dutiful Plath needs to labour like a Sisyphean curator. On the level of argument the poem has a Kafkaesque gloom. As the pointless and irrational labour stretches endlessly into the future, the boat she has hoped will take her away is no longer even listened for. Yet as so often in Plath – and, indeed, in early Barthes – a dismal argument is contradicted by a language which drags the idea in different directions. Thus 'The Colossus' spits an insolent insubordination at the same time as it shackles the speaker to her labour. The diction muddles Roman antiquity and household implements ('gluepots and pails of Lysol'), and the voice of the (male) oracle becomes a verbal farmyard: 'Mule-bray, pig-grunt and bawdy cackles'. The disconcerting mixture of pain and irony is both gender- and period-specific, and Plath's language seems to me to be working in much the same way as Barthes describes in *Writing Degree Zero* – that is, it is the language and form which primarily enact the resistance to an orthodoxy which the argument depressingly seems to sustain.

As is common in Barthes, *Writing Degree Zero* mixes the gloomy and the utopian. If his general account of the literary culture is crushing, the book also has a positive reflex, a sporadic holiday from convention which lies in the joy of language before its Fall into 'Literature':

> Writing, free at its beginnings, is finally the bond which links the writer to History which is itself in chains: society stamps upon him the unmistakable signs of art so as to draw him along the more inescapably in its own process of alienation. (*WDZ*, 40)

The trick, therefore, will be to discover this original freedom and a refreshed sense of existence rather than the mere husk of meaning (*WDZ*, 32). As we saw in *Michelet*, Barthes argues against transcendent evaluations of art, but this position also runs against Sartre's conception of its freedom. For Barthes, the art-work represents not freedom, but the captivity of original creativity by institutional forms, and *Writing Degree Zero* proposes an account of creativity which is again both interestingly close to, and different from, influential ideas in Britain in the period.

Barthes's model is triadic. Writing treats of three forces: language, 'Literature', and what he calls 'style'. By language he means the plentiful resources of the tongue, in all their diversity and possibility. By 'Literature' he means the forces that restrict this plenty. By style he means the individual stamp of the writer, the personal element which wrestles 'Literature' into creativity. Barthes's metaphors for style are revealingly period-specific. Style is a frontier 'to overstep which alone might lead to the linguistically supernatural'. Style springs from 'the body and the past of the writer and gradually become[s] the very reflexes of his art'. It has its roots in 'the depths of the author's personal and secret mythology, that subnature of expression where the first coition of words and things takes place, where once and for all the great verbal themes of his existence come to be installed'. It is 'crude . . . the product of a thrust . . . germinative'; it 'rises up out of the writer's myth-laden depths and unfolds beyond the area of his control . . . the decorative voice of hidden, secret flesh'. It is allusive, carnal, and 'carries man to the threshold of power and magic', far from the 'security of art' (*WDZ*, 9–12).

The first resemblance here is to the themes of the body in *Michelet*, though this kind of neo-Lawrentian, psychosexual rhapsody was common in the postwar escape from austerity and restriction. (In Britain, this was a boom time for Lawrence's reputation, especially among the young.) But this passage also resembles another form of poetic mythologising by Robert Graves, whose *The White Goddess* (first edition 1948) influenced new writers like Ted Hughes and Sylvia Plath. Graves was interested in the roots of personal mythology, and he too described the carnality which lies at its core. The figure of the white goddess is a kind of emblem for the origin of poetry in the deep layers of the bodily psyche. It thus represents psychological and spiritual experience of great importance, an ancient and violent wisdom which resists the 'capricious experiments in philosophy, science and industry' of the modern period.[9] Graves's argument, therefore, overlaps with Leavisite celebrations of the 'organic' spontaneity of art as opposed to the 'mechanical' spoliations of modern society; and Barthes, too, is hostile to capitalist culture, emphasising the alternative 'frontier' of stylistic passion. In other words, he shares a contemporary problematic for poetry with some unlikely comrades.

Or does he? More than one critic notes Barthes's paradoxical relish for style and Michelet's bodily thematics.[10] Style in *Writing Degree Zero* is an evanescent entity coloured by metaphor, but it is difficult to establish its meaning with much precision. Though he toys with a biological-mythological register in the manner of Graves, Barthes makes it clear elsewhere that he has in mind 'only' an experience of *language*. Here, we find a problem which Barthes's writing poses continually. He frequently insists on the importance of metaphor for capturing fugitive literary experiences which conventional criticism neglects. But it is difficult, especially in demanding books of high theory like *Writing Degree Zero*, to estimate the argumentative value of Barthes's metaphors. In this case, it is as if his metaphors for style deny the main thrust of his argument, rather as, he claims, happens in Michelet. Above, I quoted *Writing Degree Zero* to the effect that it is writing which eventually bonds the writer to history 'which is itself in chains'. Perhaps it is Barthes's own verbal skittishness which here connects him most closely to his fellow prisoners.

Barthes calls his ideal writing 'zero degree' writing because it resists 'Literature' so thoroughly that it enables a pure, undistracted experience of language. His model for the zero degree in prose at this point is the work of Albert Camus, for which he was an early, and orthodox Sartrean, enthusiast.[11] In poetry his models are the unspecified heirs of Mallarmé. The hallmark of the zero degree (the term originates in linguistics) is an avoidance of both 'Literature' and ordinary communication in a narrowly functional sense. Zero degree writing 'destroys the spontaneously functional nature of language' (*WDZ*, 46). It strips out emotional declaration and conceptual meaning, because these are points at which the pressure of 'Literature' might be exerted. It almost evacuates style itself: 'a style of absence which is almost an ideal absence of style', he remarks of Camus, and might have remarked of Beckett (*WDZ*, 77). It is a kind of classicism – impersonal, moral (because it sides with no ideology) and, important in existential terms, free (*WDZ*, 77–8). Barthes evocatively describes it as 'white writing'. So there is an aporia in *Writing Degree Zero*. On the one hand there is the sweaty language of style; on the other the cool classicism of the zero degree. The two modes repeat the contrast between *Michelet* and *Writing Degree Zero* themselves. The one seems to owe its origin to the humanist psychogenetics of the deep creative process, while the model for the other is the colourless austerity of linguistics. But actually, on Barthes's own account, the former must come first. It is the genetics of the creative act itself. Therefore, the logic of the argument must suggest that, under modern conditions, this volatile, original creativity has to disown its passion. The writer has to cultivate a self-negating abstinence which denies wider human engagements, and it is hard not to see in the zero degree an anorexia of language whose spartan deliberation seals the writer into a self-authenticating alienation. In 1955 Camus, Barthes's exemplar of the zero degree in prose, wrote to him to reject the direction of his arguments because they might lead to abolition of a community 'which nothing in history has so far been able to touch'.[12]

One way of considering this aporia is historically. Barthes's zero degree can be understood as a postwar wish for verbal hygiene uncluttered by propaganda and other wartime distortions. Such desires are common. In Britain they were a leading motivation for I.A. Richards's 'practical criticism' after World War I, and Orwell wrote in similar ways around World War II. These circumstances go some way towards contextualising Barthes's Cold War pessimism. But his formalism remains in awkward alterity with the warmer humanism of his characteristic 1950s vision of the passionate mythic style, and here again Barthes rejoins the general argument. If, for Graves and his acolytes, literature represented a consolation for marginality in modern industrial culture, then the zero degree can be seen in the same light. Modern poetry, Barthes writes, destroys the functionality of language. It 'leaves standing only its lexical basis', and 'this void is necessary for the density of the Word to rise out of a magic vacuum, like sound and a sign devoid of background, like "fury and mystery"' (*WDZ*, 46–7). The first, violent image is that of a bombed city; the second shifts towards the mythic: modern poetry strips out the syntactical and semantic connectives; it is 'left only with a vertical project, it is like a monolith, or a pillar . . . it is a sign which stands' (*WDZ*, 47). This Stonehenge of poetry has stopped being a zero, an absence, and has turned back again into a substantive, mythic discourse, and these phallic verticalities are of the same discursive register as the thrusting coition of style we noted above.

At the heart of Barthes's early work, therefore, is another typical 1950s motif, that of aggressive masculine sexuality. Indeed, it is arguable that the whole existential mode is a characteristically male discourse. Describing his discovery of his poetic vocation, Thom Gunn – a British writer who was also influenced by Sartre, and whom it would be interesting to consider in Barthesian terms – later wrote that 'writing poetry became the act of an existentialist conqueror, excited and aggressive'.[13] Much of this mood is observable in Osborne, Hughes, Camus and others. It is the flipside of the emphasis on cultural power against which so many of these writers saw themselves as embattled. So, alongside the monoliths of *Writing Degree Zero*, its thrusts and pillars of style, it is necessary to put the broken giant's statue of Plath's Colossus. The zero degree does not negate all of Barthes's history.

Writing Degree Zero, then, shares many of the characteristic assumptions and motifs of its period. But there is one it sets out consciously to overturn. Barthes's debt to Sartre is complex, but the engagement with Sartrean existentialism in *Writing Degree Zero* is critical. Barthes's book analyses the relationship between the writer and the available language. It is essentially a description of the *production* of writing. Sartre's *What is Literature?* (on which *Writing Degree Zero* is closely modelled), however, has a very

different basis: it is rooted in an analysis of the relationship between writer, text and reader. In other words, it is not a produc-
tional but a *transactional* model. According to Sartre, a writer does
two things. First, she or he opens the world up so that the reader
'may assume full responsibility before the object which has thus
been laid bare'.[14] Sartre's analysis is therefore content-centred, not
formalistic like Barthes's. But second – and this is much the more
impressive argument – writer, reader and text are involved in a
detailed existential transaction. The writing of the text is an appeal
to the reader; the reading of it is a creative response to the invita-
tion. The currency of these transactions is freedom, but a freedom
which is responsible both to the world (the content of literature)
and to the other partner in the process. The writer does not
'overwhelm' the reader, because that would limit the reader's freedom; and the reader is enjoined to read responsibly, not to 'play'
with the text. The transaction is wholehearted and generous, a
gratuitous gift exchanged by responsible partners, a microcosm of
interpersonal good faith. The result is a shared creative 'joy' and
affirmation, and an ideal definition of human relations in a philosophy many take to be merely individualistic.

Barthes, however, perceived the difficulties in the argument,
and in *Writing Degree Zero* he started to turn it round. Sartre's
model for art is benign and affirmative, whereas Barthes insists on
the coercive nature of the social and ideological context. Sartre
relies on the open existential good faith of both parties to the
literary experience, whereas Barthes assumes that reading is much
more a process of routinised production and consumption. Sartre
seems to take it as more or less axiomatic that language can reveal
the world as it is, whereas for Barthes such realism is a pernicious
delusion. Finally, Sartre's model is one of a communal exchange,
whereas for Barthes the writer's task is a lonely solitude, fundamentally 'indifferent to society' (*WDZ*, 12). Late in his career
Barthes moved towards a reconciliation of some of these differences, but a comparison with Sartre's book shows the stresses
and strains of two very different writers' engagement with existential questions, and Barthes's reversal of Sartre here establishes the
positions which he was to explore for the next twenty years.

It is sometimes asked of literary theory that it teach a 'method'.
From time to time Barthes did that, but not in *Writing Degree Zero*
or *Michelet*. If an inventory is required of the portable property

one might take from this early work, one could offer: the attack on realism; the analysis of a 'thematics' of writing in *Michelet*; and, perhaps above all, the pessimistic sense of an incorporative culture which pushes writing to the alienated margins. These, along with the formalistic emphasis on language rather than its content, will prove abiding themes for Barthes, as will the equivocation between 'hot' style and the zero degree. But to make method from these two books is perhaps not the point. They are not so much the instruments of analysis for contemporary writing as its partners. They elaborate the conceptual structure within which certain of its works are understood.

In a number of essays in this period, Barthes wrote enthusiastically of the 'nouveau roman', particularly the work of Alain Robbe-Grillet. Robbe-Grillet was a natural ally for Barthes, and the two agreed on many points of theory. Against Sartre, Robbe-Grillet also argued that writers do not have political 'engagements', or even interesting ideas. They explore their material through style and form. Both novelist and critic agreed that it was necessary for new writing to free itself from the past, and risk appearing shapeless in finding a new form. Novelists should try to eliminate the expectations of 'Literature' in such rudimentary matters as the psychological analysis of character or the description of milieu.[15] Barthes and Robbe-Grillet recommended a deliberate alienation of the reader, and the creation of perplexity as to causes and behaviour. (Both were partly led to this by their admiration for Kafka and Brecht.) Thus the interpretative signs a reader might normally look for are absent in Robbe-Grillet's novels: there is no 'character' as such, no 'setting', no metaphor, no anthropomorphism that might make the world homely. Robbe-Grillet's is a static, disorientating adventure in language; a step-by-step literalism which may or may not conceal plot (a sort of 'woz-it-dun?'). In short, all the dynamics of Sartre's transactional relationship between writer and reader are thwarted in a manner not unlike that of Harold Pinter's work in the same period, where one point of the drama is that the audience comes to understand that their own interpretative conventions and assumptions have been called into question.

These arguments have the feel of their period, just as Robbe-Grillet's novels are preoccupied by the colonial twilight, male sexual violence, and the uncertainties of changing social and sexual codes – all of which were major postwar concerns on both sides of the Channel. But they also bear upon persisting issues in yet more recent work, and have been taken up again by the Glasgow novelist James Kelman. Kelman's subject matter – life on the Glasgow housing schemes – presents serious formal challenges because, he argues, the language of working-class Glasgow cannot be written within the accepted forms of a conventional 'Literature' stuffed with stereotypes of how working-class people speak and behave. (The literary origins of fiction about the working class lie in the nineteenth-century urban-realist novel which 'presented' the life of the industrial proletariat to a middle-class readership.) Kelman therefore needs to cultivate a 'zero degree' of 'Literature' exactly in the sense intended by Barthes and Robbe-Grillet, and he acknowledges his debt to the latter. In his stories and novels, Kelman has sought to find ways of representing popular experience by resisting a literary language which would betray that effort through inappropriate, conventional plots, distorting vocabulary or imagery, or an irony which makes a knowing pact with the educated reader to the detriment of the human situation being represented.[16] The kinds of issues addressed in *Writing Degree Zero* are very much alive.

The inferno of meanings

Barthes's views were controversial, and need to be understood as such. This section will therefore examine two more of his early books, *On Racine* (1963) and *Criticism and Truth* (1966), in relation to the so-called 'Picard affair', a head-on collision between the 'Nouvelle Critique' – for which Barthes was now the most prominent spokesman – and the French critical establishment. It is sometimes claimed that the work of the 'Nouvelle Critique' has effected a 'Copernican revolution' in criticism over recent decades. Needless to say, this view is challenged by traditionalists, but it is striking how similar arguments in both French and English studies have been over such issues. This section will therefore close by looking at the hostile reception Barthes's work received in Britain and the United States in the 1970s when Barthes became, in the words of one of his critics, 'the strongest influence on American criticism today'.[17]

On Racine is a compendium book of three essays from diverse
sources, written between 1958 and 1960. The essays cover three
topics. 'Racinian man' uses modern psychoanalysis and
anthropology to give a radically new account of the dynamics of
Racine's plays which follows pretty directly from the work begun
in *Michelet*. 'Racine spoken' is a lengthy review of productions of
the plays in 1958, in which Barthes attacks contemporary styles
of acting because they reduce Racine to a group of declaimed set
speeches. The essay develops Barthes's long-standing argument
against psychological naturalism in drama. The third essay,
'History or literature?', originally published in *Annales*, is a
theoretical conspectus of the general critical positions Barthes
had advocated over the previous decade. It resumes the argument
made for a new literary history in *Writing Degree Zero*, and calls
for a study of the uses made of Racine in, for example, education,
theatrical production and the history of literary 'taste'. In short,
it is to be a case study in 'Literature'. The essay is a confrontational attack on traditional scholarship and the notion of a self-
evident literary canon. Barthes wants to understand not Racine's
'greatness', but his *function*. Literary history, he argues, is
important only in so far as it helps us to understand 'the
phenomena of collective mentality' being studied by 'Annales'
historians like Lucien Febvre (*Racine*, 160). Criticism, Barthes
brutally claims, should 'amputate literature from the individual'
(*Racine*, 162).

On Racine argues that criticism is not an antiquarian celebration
of the glories of the past. It is fundamentally contemporary, and *all*
literature issues an existential challenge to the present. 'To write is
to jeopardise the meaning of the world', Barthes remarks (*Racine*,
ix). By this he means that literature challenges and questions, it
does not provide 'art' or static values. The critic's job is to articulate his own times, to 'affirm, each on behalf of his own history and
his own freedom, the historical, or psychological, or psychoanalyt-
ical, or poetic truth of Racine' (*Racine*, x). This is Barthes at his
most existentially provocative, and *On Racine* and *Critical Essays*
(1964) together form a kind of piecemeal manifesto for modernity.
Barthes recruits certain writers (Brecht, Robbe-Grillet, Kafka,
Bataille, for example) as an alternative tradition which speaks most
directly to the present. In *On Racine* he uses these bench-marks to
reread the canonical playwright against what he calls the 'myth of

Racine', the worship of his transcendental, de-historicised genius.
The myth, Barthes argues, is:

> essentially a security operation: it seeks to domesticate Racine, to
> strip him of his tragic elements, to identify him with ourselves, to
> locate ourselves with him in the noble salon of classic art, but *en
> famille*; it seeks to give the themes of the bourgeois theatre an
> eternal status, to transfer to the credit of the psychological theatre
> the greatness of the tragic theatre, which at its origin, we must not
> forget, was a purely civic theatre: in the myth of Racine, eternity
> replaces the city. (*Racine*, 149)

Barthes claims that traditional ways of producing and thinking
about Racine tame the writer, make his great tragic theatre cosily
en famille. He wants to make him both wild and topical. The joke
about the security operation was written at the height of the devas-
tating terrorist war in French Algeria.

The first essay in the book provocatively applies the insights of
modern anthropology and psychoanalysis. Barthes argues that
Racine's plays represent a primal struggle in the sexual dynamics
of power based on the Freudian model of the 'primal horde', in
which younger members of the group struggle to establish their
identity within the patriarchal structure. The plays, therefore,
become not reverential salon pieces but dramas about fundamental
division and disunion, transgression and violence, and the psychology of unconscious compulsion and repetition. Racine's work
is an 'inferno of meanings' in which ambiguity and conflict are the
norm (*Racine*, 56). What excites Barthes is the way Racine's studied classical aesthetic collides with an ethics of primal violence
(*Racine*, 133). But, he argues, this has been accommodated and
tamed by a mixture of overawed scholarship and belletrism which
has substituted a harmless eternity of art and vapid psychology of
'character'. As the adroitly topical references in the passage quoted
above imply, Barthes reads his Racine with full existential gusto
and a severe eye on the conservative establishment in literary
studies which produces texts to reflect the cautious modesty of its
own version of classical 'genius'. Where conventional criticism
provides 'that ensemble of objects and rules, techniques and
works, whose function in the general economy of society is precisely *to institutionalize subjectivity*' (*Racine*, 172), Barthes's Racine
spills over with ideas and ambiguities, and speaks directly to a

radical subjectivity desirous of existential freedom and unalarmed at the world's divisions.[18]

It is intriguing to consider Barthes's emphasis on turmoil and rebellion in the light of his own relations with critical orthodoxy, because *On Racine* began a war within the primal horde of French critics. Most prominent among the older generation was the Racine scholar and Sorbonne professor, Raymond Picard. Picard, needled by a polemical piece Barthes wrote for the *Times Literary Supplement* that unpatriotically aired his unflattering views on French criticism before an international audience, attacked the 'Nouvelle Critique' across the board in a widely circulated pamphlet, *New Criticism or New Fraud?* (1965). For Picard, Barthes lacked respect for the text, and for literature itself. His Racine was a simple distortion. Four years after the *Lady Chatterley* trial, the characters of Barthes's Racine were little different from those of D.H. Lawrence, and there is a heavy note of moral censure throughout Picard's polemic. Barthes's work is obsessive, unbridled, cynical, intemperate, totalitarian, destructive, rash, gratuitous, delirious, perverted, fantastic, chaotic, oversexualised and duped. In opposition, Picard launches a contrastingly positive vocabulary: modest, noble, sensitive, patient, prudent, tasteful. These are the criteria of 'art'.[19] Barthes, Picard laments, is a feckless 'talent gone astray', unable to recognise the essential differences in things. Psychoanalysis, for instance, is for patients, not literature; and writers are geniuses, not unconscious automata. Literary creation is careful, conscious and coherent, whereas Barthes's Racine is the automatic writing of the surrealist avant-garde. Racine's plays 'have a literal meaning which was obligatory', and one cannot simply make things up at a later date. Barthes therefore ignores 'reality itself', and creates a literary promiscuity in which all writers are the heirs of modernism and surrealism. His ostensible scientificity is a purely metaphorical way of concealing a radical and sceptical subjectivism driven by naked ideology and the 'spirit of system'.

Despite the notoriety of his pamphlet, Picard was not a successful polemicist. There is little wit in his prose, and Barthes trounced his efforts in this respect. Instead, he relies on one or two good, but repeated, arguments (about Barthes's spurious scientificity, for instance, or his lack of a historical sense of the text) and on efficiently mobilising the conservative consensus. A vocabulary which relies on

words like noble and tasteful depends very much upon its audience's acceptance that these words have meaning and value in this
context. The wide-ranging quarrel that ensued in the press and
across the literary-academic world was about this kind of issue, and
Barthes was right to see it as essentially an issue of language. This
was certainly the view of Serge Doubrovsky, whose *Pourquoi la
nouvelle critique?: critique et objectivité* (1966) – translated as *The New
Criticism in France* – is perhaps the best book to have come out of
the whole business. Doubrovsky, a not uncritical pro-Barthesian
phenomenologist, set the context for a debate whose importance was
revealed by the speed with which it spread and the depth of antagonism it revealed. The view that literature was reasonable, calm,
clear, noble, and so forth, Doubrovsky noted, was undoubtedly the
view of 'good society' which is prone to admire its own clichés, but
the real issue (as Barthes also claimed in *Criticism and Truth*, his
riposte to Picard) is the taboo this language puts on other ideas. It is
in effect, Doubrovsky wrote, 'a machinery of censorship' which
substitutes 'the pledge of an eternal hierarchy of truths and values'
for open discussion and debate.[20]

Doubrovsky's book is impressive for a number of reasons. It
works carefully through Barthes's polemic (which had rather mud-
dled some issues), but above all it has an unusually well-informed
command of the international context and a clear-headed sense of
the wider issues at stake. These were nothing less than the whole
issue of modernisation, especially in education, which was being
faced across the West in the early 1960s. In Britain Harold Wilson
had just won the 1964 General Election for Labour by playing just
this modernisation card – the 'white heat of the technological revolution', as he famously called it – but Doubrovsky compared the
Barthes–Picard quarrel to that about the teaching of the new mathematics then being introduced in the United States. Fundamentally,
the debate was really about modern educational methods and a
conception of teaching and learning which was not locked into the
past. Picard – whom Doubrovsky explicitly compared to the American New Critics of the 1930s – was wedded to a view that learning is
a matter of passive reception, that knowledge is a stable hierarchy of
rules and values, that literary texts have singular stable meanings,
and that scholarly objectivity is unproblematic. To put it simply,
Picard was ill-informed about modern linguistics and theories of
knowledge, and one cannot, Doubrovsky claims, base education on

antique ideas. The whole spirit of modern knowledge, he argues, is founded on 'radical questioning'; and in literature, meaning exists 'in suspense', awaiting activation by specific, historically positioned readers. Literature, in this sense, has no eternal truths (Doubrovsky, 237, 269–72).

Doubrovsky argues from a thoroughgoing existential-phenomenological position which again owes much to Sartre. He holds that literary meaning is created between individuals. It is a historical and psychological event and is not established once and for all, as Picard is inclined to claim. Meaning changes over time, depending on historical and personal circumstances. Here Barthes would be much in agreement. However, Doubrovsky is critical of Barthes's formalism. He argues that Barthes is interested only in the formal properties of language, not in the content of what is said. For Doubrovsky this significantly shrinks literature's range and value, and compromises its full plurality by restraining its direct involvement with the world. In an odd way, Doubrovsky notes, Barthes and Picard resemble each other: both overvalue a certain mode of language use (Racine's classicism or the avant-garde zero degree) at the expense of what is being said, and both construct a canon of major writers – in Barthes's case the modernist canon of Kafka, Brecht, Robbe-Grillet and the rest – which is used as a dogmatic standard for judgement (Doubrovsky, 139–46). For Doubrovsky, therefore, Barthes is not phenomenological *enough*. Like Camus, Doubrovsky is impatient with a view of literature which reduces it to the spectacle of language chasing in circles like squirrels in a cage 'for the delectation of observing linguists' (Doubrovsky, 150). Barthes's dogmatism about the purity of language contradicts his much better argument for literature's power to question and unsettle (Doubrovsky, 143).

In his own reply to Picard, *Criticism and Truth* (1966), Barthes also emphasised the language question, and recognised the importance of the 'modernisation' argument. In an interview in 1965 he claimed that it was he, not Picard, who was 'the real guardian of national values' because he was making the classics available to a modern audience (*Grain*, 41). But it is the issue of a viable critical language which dominates a book largely given over to exposing the mendacities and blind spots of the traditional critical lexicon. *Criticism and Truth* is a witty exposé of the hidden meanings of customary critical vocabulary, and it reads a little like a high-flown version of newspaper articles which ironically 'translate' the euphemisms of estate agents or advertisers into their 'real' meanings. Thus the real meaning of critical 'objectivity' is that one ignores ambiguities or multiple meanings and pretends that one's own position is calmly neutral, whereas those of others are partisan and ill-informed (*Criticism*, 36–9). Similarly, 'good taste' is not an infallible instinct for quality, but a prohibition against other kinds of language. Clarity, rather than a communicative instrument, is a 'sacred idiom' which rules out certain forms of expression. In one of the book's running images, it is compared to a kind of ablution or hygiene of language used to flush out unwanted elements or a 'kind of terminological miner's claim' on correct opinion (*Criticism*, 49). In short, Barthes accuses traditional criticism of 'asymbolia', a language disorder in which sufferers are unable to manipulate the full resources of the tongue. Barthes's own language, by contrast, becomes increasingly extravagant and, as Doubrovsky noticed, his ideas sometimes seem to have their very existence only in the metaphorical glow given by his witty harangue of the establishment. *Criticism and Truth* is very successful polemic against an increasingly weak-looking traditionalism, and it has an alert eye to its own historical context. But it is hard not to feel, with Doubrovsky, that certain important issues to do with the content and substance of literature and education are being finessed, and to agree with Picard that the claim to scientificity made at length in the final part of the book is somewhat bogus.

The questions raised by the Picard quarrel have in a sense never been resolved, and contemporary educational discussion frequently returns to versions of the debate about learning by questioning or learning by rule. But in the mid-1960s there was no doubt which way the future lay. The 'Nouvelle Critique' seemed much more responsive to the needs of the moment than what seemed to be backward-looking, conservative recommendations of modesty and prudence. The quarrel about literary meaning, however, was playing out a larger dispute. It is now widely accepted that one important dimension of it was the interinstitutional struggle for authority between Picard's high-status, traditionalist Sorbonne and Barthes's new-fangled, underrecognised École Pratique des Hautes Études. The sociologist Pierre Bourdieu goes further. For him, the Picard affair was fought on an already established 'field of conflict' in French intellectual culture between two generations of academic: the establishment Picard and the more belligerently marginal Barthes. Whatever the detailed issues of substance between them, the lines of force which engineered the quarrel had more substantial origins in the divisions and circumstances of French society.[21]

Structural factors like these play a major role in the dynamics of explosive incidents, but it is striking that the kinds of issues that were addressed in the Picard affair transcend national boundaries. Indeed, it is the very internationalism of what was taken to be Barthes's outlook which dictated much of the character of his early reception in Britain. Some work has already been done on his reception in the United States,[22] but little has been done to draw an equivalent picture on the other side of the Atlantic. What follows, therefore, is an attempt to look at corresponding reactions in Britain, and what is striking is a significant correlation between the arguments launched against Barthes's work in France, the UK and the USA alike. The defence of 'real' literature launched by Picard in his attack on *On Racine* is mirrored by the wish to resist the 'modernising' culture of the 1960s by critics like Gerald Graff in the USA and less gifted thinkers in Britain.[23]

In Britain the defence of literature has been conducted as a defence of a traditional national culture and a resistance to the international traffic of ideas. The context for this is the alteration in cultural perspective which has accompanied the technological, political and economic transformations of recent decades. The expansion and diversity of the student population, the growth of an increasingly 'cultured' audience, the enlargement of the affluent market for cultural products – the new, and often international – modes of cultural access (especially television), the decreasing deference towards traditional cultural authorities, as well as alterations in the role and social relations of artists and intellectuals and the profound changes in the technological means of producing written and other cultural forms, from book production to electronic communications systems – all these have altered the infrastructural conditions for criticism beyond those imaginable when its traditional protocols were established. It is these changes which have, in the end, transported Barthes's 'inferno of meanings' across more than two seas.

Reading through hostile British responses to Barthes's work, one is struck by the way they return to a handful of repeated themes. Barthes had early been identified with the international avant-garde. A prominent review of *Critical Essays* appears, for instance, in the first of the *Times Literary Supplement*'s two special numbers on the European and American avant-garde in 1964. Though the reviewer was puzzled as to 'the ultimate values behind M. Barthes's pattern of significance',[24] surrounding work by Miroslav Holub, Max Bense, Marshall McLuhan, Allen Ginsberg, Eduardo Paolozzi, Ian Hamilton Finlay, Richard Hamilton and others made the connections clear. The *Supplement*'s editorials, meanwhile, in the year of Wilson's election victory, spelt out the 'modernisation' argument once more. Though traditional British virtues had their worth, culture was now international and the avant-garde was essential.[25] By contrast, the opening of an antagonistic book on Barthes by Philip Thody (a professor of French) takes one aback: Barthes is 'so extraordinary when looked at from this side of the Channel that one often wonders . . . whether phrases about "a common European culture" have any meaning at all'.[26] So here is the first theme: that Barthes is alien and odd, and somewhat untrustworthy. Like Picard, commentators speak of his grotesqueness, his narcissism, his irrationality, his flightiness and dandyism, his deviousness, and the 'vices' of his work. According to another professor of French, Geoffrey Strickland, these vices are typical of French intellectuals in general.[27]

A number of these commentators salute Picard directly, and one – Peter Washington – honours his pamphlet in the title of his book: *Fraud*. But the resemblances of argument and accusation are more important: Barthes is overingenious, but unsophisticated, merely fashionable and dogmatic, obscure and overgeneralising, dictatorial and overbearing. More importantly, it is held that he opposes proper literature, which is a special category remote from modern mass culture or psychoanalytic theory. His work is trivial and destructive of quality writing. It dissects, breaks into fragments, X-rays, manhandles, or otherwise damages by intellectualising the precious wholes of poetry with an arbitrary oversimplification and scepticism which refuse to engage with the ordinary world of common reference (this is an attack on Barthes's anti-realism). Most important of all, however, is the destruction it wreaks on the literary canon and, by extension, the common culture. What is really corrosive about Barthes's work, claim Holloway, Parrinder, Scruton, Strickland, Thody and Washington, is its dismissal of objectivity and truth, and a shared sense of what binds society together. Barthes, in refusing a clear conception of shared history and interests, refuses the critic's proper role as a transmitter of cultural conventions, tastes and values, all of which have their best representation in literature. It is not difficult to see the connection with that cultural capital Barthes called 'Literature'.

Some of these arguments misrepresent Barthes's views (for instance, over popular culture), and clearly none shares his politics, hazy though these are. What is also striking is that these attacks mobilise a range of polemical argument and language which has been extraordinarily persistent in British culture since the mid-nineteenth century, when almost identical positions and imagery were used by opponents of the new evolutionary psychology, which was also thought to be tainted by French revolutionary scepticism.[28] But what is most at issue is an attitude to criticism and literature and the role they play in modern life, and here points made by Serge Doubrovsky in the early 1960s still hold good. The argument about common cultures, for instance, made in the traditional way, seems implausible in a world in which notions of secure national traditions are being eroded by increasingly international circumstances and frames of reference. This does not mean that these arguments no longer have purchase on elements of the existing political culture in Britain, but it does mean that they no longer recognise the increasingly polyglot nature of cultural attitudes and international methods of cultural production. While this or that position taken by Barthes may arguably be false or misjudged, the outlook of his criticism, in responding to a changed cultural environment, is one with which we still need to work.

In Britain, during the ideological polarities of the 1970s and 1980s, there was a collusion by both Left and Right to claim that literary or cultural 'theory' is separate. For Rightist critics, modern theory is frequently portrayed as either laughably erroneous or a debased version of a more robust native product. Thus, for Philip Thody, Barthes is a poor relation of Orwell in his commentaries on popular culture, and his criticism is 'not in the same league' as that of G. Wilson Knight, F.R. Leavis or L.C. Knights (who, extraordinarily, is said to anticipate the entire argument of Barthes's *S/Z*). This habit of comparative denigration is widespread, and serves to render trivial and unnecessary the work of more modern thinkers. On the Left, meanwhile, continental theory has been trumpeted as the answer to many ills and, following the lead of Perry Anderson's *New Left Review* and New Left Books in the late 1960s, it has been consciously imported to fill what was pictured as a domestic void. This strange agreement that theory is extraneous has had the effect of separating ideas from context and from each other by insisting that what is 'over there' is different. Perhaps it is time we started to think about things in a wider frame.

Mythography: structuralist analysis and popular culture

In a short book it is easy to pull a writer's career out of shape, particularly when there is a large number of preconceptions about his or her reputation. This is especially the case with writers whose work is influential in a language not their own, for the chronology of the career is often distorted by the delays (or absence) of translation. Though Barthes has been lucky in his translators, Elizabeth Bruss argues in *Beautiful Theories* that the Anglo–American sense of his work has been skewed in its reception.[1] The appearance *en masse* in the early 1970s of translations of and commentaries on his work, as well as that of important contemporaries like the anthropologist Claude Lévi-Strauss, created the impression that Barthes was the doyen of 'structuralism', a fully formed 'scientific' methodology whose fruits had only to be picked by tardy English-speaking critics. In fact, Barthes's 'structuralist phase' never happened in these terms, and his most celebrated reputation is probably spurious.[2] Although he did work with structuralist ideas for a time from the late 1950s to the late 1960s, it is essential not to isolate this period. A number of recent commentators have argued that Barthes's structuralism, as well as resuming earlier themes, contains a number of his later anti-structuralist positions.[3] None the less, it is necessary to understand something of structuralism to see what Barthes did with it. This chapter will therefore begin with a brief account of structuralism before examining its applications in the second section, and, in the last, commenting on important parallels and differences from contemporary work in Britain.

Theory

What is now usually known as structuralism was developed in the late 1950s in France from international sources. As a mode of enquiry, structural analysis is as old as thinking itself and has encompassed, from time to time, intellectual disciplines from philosophy to the hard sciences. The major thinkers of 'Parisian' structuralism were, in addition to Barthes, Claude Lévi-Strauss, an anthropologist; Jacques Lacan, a psychoanalyst; Louis Althusser, a Marxist philosopher; and Michel Foucault, an anti-Marxist philosopher and historian. The structuralism of all these thinkers has two ideas in common. The first idea proposes that the nature of individual things or persons is determined by their place in a larger structure, be this social, psychological, political, literary, or whatever. The second proposes that this apparently harmless conception requires a fundamental reorientation of our understanding. Instead of starting with the individual and working outwards to understand the world (a mental map which was sometimes said by structuralists to be pre-Copernican because it puts humanity at the centre of the universe), structuralism begins from the structure and appears to picture human beings, literary texts or historical occurrences as incidental and, indeed, predictable features produced by larger, impersonal forces. This is what made structuralism controversial.[4]

Many modern structuralists took language itself as their basic model for the operation of these general structures, and it is easy to see why. Language is an appropriate model because individual utterances in any language cannot be made without an enabling structure to give them meaning. The meaning of this sentence, like that of any other sentence in English, is able to signify because it follows the structural rules of the language. The operation of language, therefore, seemed to many, including Barthes, to be an apt model for all cultural phenomena, from myth to modern fashion. The language model has a satisfying complexity, a kind of universality (all cultures have one) and a quasi-scientific prestige borrowed from linguistics.

The fountainhead of the model favoured by modern structuralists was the Swiss linguist, Ferdinand de Saussure, whose turn-of-the-century work, though it is now controversial (in part because of the exorbitant claims made for it by later partisans), founded the modern conception of how language functions. Indeed, it was this emphasis on the functionality of language which was the key notion in structuralist developments of Saussure. Instead of examining a language's historical evolution, Saussure tried to understand how language *worked*. Again, the implications of this, at first sight, rather obvious advance are considerable, because by switching attention to how things function rather than what they are worth (every community is proud of its own language), structuralism entertains a relativism of values which offends some people. Structuralism is, in principle, indifferent to cultural value because it is concerned with how things function. This is why, for Barthes, it seemed a suitable means of analysing popular culture in a period racked by uncertainties about the new 'mass' society.

Saussure's work is, of course, more complex than any quick summary can show, but it pivots on a number of basic analytic distinctions.[5] For our purposes, the foremost among these is that between *langue* and *parole*, the language system and the individual utterance. Saussure's analysis is pitched towards *langue*, the structure which must be prior to any actual language use, because he is trying to give an account of the functional conditions of meaning. He also distinguishes between *synchronic* and *diachronic* ways of studying language. A synchronic study examines the structural conditions of language at any given moment, while diachronic study looks at its historical development. Obviously enough, structural analysis concentrates on the synchronic: the functional relationships within the system which enable language to work.

Furthermore, because language is seen in an entirely functional perspective, individual *signs* are considered not to have a 'natural' relationship with what are usually called their *referents* (the things, actions, ideas or relationships they designate in the world outside language). Because language is a functioning mechanism, its individual units are arbitrary in the sense that they are only conventional. The meanings of even basic words are therefore theoretically alterable. In Saussurean theory, there is no reason outside historical circumstance why the object before you should be called *a book* rather than *un livre*. All that *functionally* matters is that the sign 'book' is different from all other signs. It is therefore the difference between signs, not the identity of sign and referent, which is the important feature. Why we call this a book (and not a nook, rook, look, or any other word in the language) is merely a matter of convention and difference. Saussure therefore divided the individual sign into two: the *signifier* (the acoustic or graphic element) and the *signified* (the mental concept conventionally associated with it). This radical separation of the mental idea from the referent, and the material basis of the sign from its mental concept, appealed enormously to those, like Barthes, who opposed a 'realist' view of language. (A 'realist' view of language would involve the belief that there was a sufficiently direct connection between words and things; that language mirrored, rather than constructed, 'real life'. As we saw in Chapter 1, Barthes opposed such beliefs.)

There are other fundamental features of Saussure's conception of language to which we will need to return as we proceed, but even from this brief account it is easy to see that its implications can be unsettling. For the most part, we rely on language so intimately, and wield it so unselfconsciously, that we tend to think of it as obedient and reliable, like muscle power or sight. But in fact it is a social construction, and therefore susceptible to misuse or manipulation. Language is not a natural instrument; the world is constructed by it, not the other way round. Throughout his career, Barthes insisted that conventions always have designs upon us and try to persuade us of the legitimacy of the *status quo*, so it is easy to see why Saussurean theory should be attractive to him. It seemed to provide ideas which could develop, with the exactitude of science, the kinds of insights he had articulated in his early work, for the structuralist view of language corresponds to the monolithic conception of 'Literature' in *Writing Degree Zero*. We need the conventions of 'Literature', just as we need the conventions of language, because they enable us to articulate the world. But, Barthes argued, we have to resist its enormous coercions; and once again, for him, individuals are pitched against a huge system on which they none the less depend. This double-bind is at the root of much of Barthes's work.

The structuralist development of Saussure's work uses it in ways that are only latent in the original. But Saussure did look to the future in one sense: he envisaged 'semiology', the study of all sign systems, on the same principles as the study of language. Barthes's extrapolation from Saussure was therefore encouraged at a time when the new communications technologies were evolving a thousandfold. Before moving to a closer discussion of Barthes's work in this area, it is worth pondering some of the problems the structuralist model presents, because these shape not only his use but also his eventual rejection of it. These limitations suggest why structuralism has few enthusiastic partisans today, and why it would be safe to say that its theoretical reorientations (towards system, function and structure rather than the value of the individual unit) have been more influential than its analytic techniques.

There are a number of basic objections. The first concerns the alienation of language from its users, and two arguments oppose the structuralist view: first, it is said that there are in fact 'deep' language structures wired into the brain which make it a more humanly immediate and less alienated system than structuralists suppose; second, even if language is radically arbitrary in origin, it is not so in use, and the creative use of familiar materials makes language a versatile and enabling system rather than one which crudely imposes its conventionality. Structuralist appropriations of Saussure assume a malign conception of the language community. Thus human creativity, moral debate, instrumental co-operation – indeed, the many dimensions of human agency itself – are devalued and ignored. As a result, because of its commitment to 'synchronic' analysis and neglect of historical variety, structuralism has a real problem explaining change or growth. What started as a methodological imperative towards synchronic analysis in Saussure (whose work was unfinished) has been converted into a hopeless existential trap. By its concentration on brute functionality, structuralist analysis is unable to offer adequate accounts of phenomena which demand much more complex responses – for instance, those required by sophisticated literary texts. As we shall see, this kind of problem troubled Barthes consistently, and was a reason for abandoning structuralist theory.

Barthes's work in his 'high'-structuralist manner consists of three books – *Mythologies* (1957), *Elements of Semiology* (1964) and *The Fashion System* (1967) – and a number of important essays, principally 'An introduction to the structural analysis of narratives' (1966). Of these, we will look here at *Elements of Semiology* and *The Fashion System* before moving, in the next section, to consider possible applications of Barthes's structuralism in more detail.

Elements of Semiology is a state-of-the-art primer of semiotic theory. Its title deliberately echoed André Martinet's *Elements of General Linguistics* (1960), at that time the most influential manual of linguistic theory in France.[6] Barthes's *Elements* is a tough read; it is austerely technical in outlook and, like *The Fashion System*, cultivates a rhetorical carapace of scientificity which, as we shall see, is somewhat at odds with some features of its argument. But *Elements of Semiology* is a lucidly composed exposition of the post-Saussurean developments described above. The introduction makes a brief case for the importance of semiology as a new analytic method for the era of mass communications before moving to an exploration of the utility of linguistic concepts for semiology. Barthes wants to establish a 'trans-linguistics' (*Elements*, 11), an interdisciplinary analysis of all signifying phenomena using the same unifying model. This would provide, as he puts it later, an account of 'the collective field of imagination of the epoch' (*Elements*, 32). In short, what Barthes is after in the *Elements* is a totalised synchronic account of culture which would match the totalised historical (or diachronic) account of the development of 'Literature' given in *Writing Degree Zero*.

So in *Elements of Semiology* we have a characteristic feature of Barthes's writing – a close attention to argumentative detail, but within a framework which is ambitiously generalising. For all its concentration on the conceptual microclimate of semiology, it is the desire for a global map which organises the book. As with much structuralist theory, it is the larger term (*langue* rather than *parole*, for instance) which has Barthes's attention. Thus *Elements*, like *Writing Degree Zero*, offers an interpretation of an existential and political condition rather than tools ('elements') for functional analysis. *Elements of Semiology* and *The Fashion System* together portray an alarming, consumer-capitalist dystopia. It is a world ostensibly without cultural values, organised by structures of routine desire for clothes, food, cars and furniture, and a corresponding absence of creativity or oppositional values. In an extraordinary passage, Barthes portrays a 'universal semanticization' of the world in a network of crisscrossing meaning systems beyond which 'there is no reality'. The functional world resides where the 'relations of the technical and the significant are woven together' (*Elements*, 42) – that is, in the heads of 'system consumers (readers; that is to say)' who receive and transmit in various systems according to their level of acculturation (*Elements*, 46). The violence of 'acculturation', then, as in *Writing Degree Zero*, is Barthes's real theme.

In Barthes's view this scenario requires a response every bit as totalised. If he diagnoses a semiological prison-house, then the radical response should be similarly massive. Accordingly, Barthes recommends a 'total ideological description' (*Elements*, 46) of the culture to 'rediscover the articulations which men impose on reality' (*Elements*, 57). Semiology will describe how reality is divided up, given meaning and then 'naturalized', as if culture were nature itself (*Elements*, 63–4). This is the ambition of structuralist semiology: to understand the functional apparatus of the semiological *langue* and to start a 'historical anthropology' of how meanings are meshed together to cover reality (*Elements*, 91). But Barthes is not aiming simply to release reality from the prison of culture. Like 'Literature', language is necessary, but it must be mobile. Once it freezes or hardens, then ideology sets in. The same must be true of semiology, and Barthes is aware that semiology, once launched, like new literary writing in *Writing Degree Zero*, will itself begin to be absorbed by the acculturative system. This being so, the only recourse is to an escalating series of dismantlings and revisions of the interpretative apparatus which will preserve its critical edge. As he puts it in *The Fashion System*, a relentless 'semiology of semiologists' (*Fashion*, 234) is required to ensure the self-consciousness which keeps the analyst on his toes. The daunting scale of this enterprise perhaps explains the strangely cautious ending to *Elements of Semiology*, the reserved tone of which is somewhat at odds with semiological ambition.

Though they are eleven years apart, it is easy to see how *Elements of Semiology* and *Writing Degree Zero* are related. Taken together, these two books (which are often published together) constitute the synchrony and diachrony of Barthes's early acculturative model. As we have seen, however, Barthes is nothing if not a restless thinker, and there is a somewhat different dynamic in *Elements* which runs counter to its explicit argument. The book's dominant metaphors are drawn from mathematics, algebra, the making of formulae, economics and, of course, linguistics. These create a patina of scientific precision. But it is striking that, from Saussure onwards, semiology has always been a science only in prospect. In *Elements of Semiology* Barthes proposes 'arthrology', a mixture of semiology and taxonomy (the study of classifications). 'Arthrology' will examine the cognitive 'grid' which humans impose on reality; and this, of course, is an importantly consistent critical project for Barthes. But it is doubtful whether the prospect of this off-the-cuff 'science' offers more than a projective rationalisation of work already begun.

In a later interview, Barthes was hard on the rhetorical tactics he himself indulges in some of his early work. 'What is fundamentally unacceptable to me', he remarks, 'is scientism; i.e. the scientific discourse which considers itself as science but refuses to consider itself as discourse. There is only one way to make the work into a dialectic: through a readiness to write, to enter into the movement of writing' (*Grain*, 81). In Chapter 3 we shall examine this kind of movement in Barthes's thought in more detail, but for the moment it is enough to understand that in *Elements of Semiology* Barthes's 'scientism' needs qualification. The text's authoritative tone is blurred by the author's awareness that totalising theories eliminate the very variety they wish to defend. Barthes's contradiction is that he protests against the incorporations of 'Literature' and ideology, but proposes a method which is equally enclosing. Structures of meaning, he comments, 'cannot admit of a continuous differential', but must insist on unilateral systems (*Elements*, 53). The paradox is that semiology – the system which displays the systems of meaning – must be similarly driven towards a theoretical monologue. Thus Barthes notes that the forms of analysis proposed by modern linguistics are 'both necessary and transitory . . . a particular taxonomy meant to be swept away by history, after having been true for a moment' (*Elements*, 82); and he concludes the volume by admitting that the technical formulae selected in it are 'purely operative and inevitably in part arbitrary' (*Elements*, 98).

On this reading, the book's 'operative' rhetoric is contradictory. It proposes 'science' while qualifying its claims, and presses ahead with Saussure's concepts as it registers their unsatisfactoriness. In his discussion of the *langue/parole* distinction, for instance, Barthes notes its advantages: it stresses sociality, the power of unconscious convention, and systematic function; it powerfully integrates with modern ideas in philosophy, psychoanalysis, anthropology, and so on (*Elements*, 23–32). But it also downgrades individual language use (the notion of individual 'style' remains important for Barthes) and, worst of all, the model is undeviatingly controlling: *langue* controls *parole*. At this point the semiotician's *langue* looks uncomfortably like the academician's 'Literature'. What happens, Barthes muses, to languages which are, of their very nature, transgressive: 'notably certain forms of literary discourse'? (*Elements*, 23) And furthermore, if everything in *langue* is so rigid, how does change or new work come about?

Barthes's metaphors now take on an interesting colouration. He speaks of 'zones' and 'frontiers' of language, as though he is now imagining language not as science but as a reflection of the Cold War partitions of middle Europe. What troubles Barthes on a theoretical level is being projected through the lens of a political situation. Concepts which may have validity at the local level of the sign lose their grip as the units of discourse get larger and the density of signification acquires a greater formal freedom. The rules which bind the organisation of sound in language are not directly applicable to the rules which organise the development of literary discourse. The problem for structuralism is that it wishes to make the whole system uniform. But the fact that large units have a density of meaning, the fact that there is a signifying abundance beyond the mere message in many forms of writing, the fact that individuals can, within limits, choose with a degree of freedom not available at the properly 'linguistic' level of the phoneme – all this permits 'the inventiveness of the "poetic" zone of speech', and this is a matter for style alone (*Elements*, 70). Barthes's response to modern consumer culture, therefore, is split between the cold confrontation of 'total ideological description' and the cultivation of the hot 'zones' of language in literature. In the long run, as we shall see in Chapter 3, it is the latter course which Barthes eventually pursues. The former is too heartbreaking.

Metaphors, as Barthes well knew, both illustrate and disclose, and the difference between the language of science and the language of zones and frontiers seems to me to represent an alteration of perspective which is central to his work. In his structuralism, as in *Writing Degree Zero*, the weight of attention is towards the icy structures that girdle the hot zone of semantic fertility which is

literary style. In *The Fashion System*, this produces a frank pessimism in a text which – rarely for Barthes – is unable to handle the
transition from theory to materials with much grace or finesse.
The details of the fashion system are crunched by a solemn theoretical machine which recognises the remorseless invention of the
'pseudo-real' in fashion magazines, but mainly forgets their fri-
volity and irony. Fashion, language, literature – *The Fashion System* presents them all as the engineering of constraint: a 'tyranny',
in one of its favourite Cold War words. In the book's habitual
metaphors, fashion is an endless roundabout of circuits, networks
and pathways which is 'simultaneously imposed and demanded
. . . where a singular (or oligarchical) conception and a collective
image meet' (*Fashion*, 215). Like many on the Left in this period,
Barthes is struck by the complicity of 'the mass' in their own
cultural impoverishment. But he fails to distinguish between the
commercial and the popular, and between what is sold and what
people do with it. He further fails to recognise what people do
apart from buying.

The Fashion System* was begun, as an academic thesis, in 1957;
finished, according to Barthes's Foreword, in 1963; and published
in 1967. It unmistakably echoes another structuralist classic –
Michel Foucault's *The Order of Things*, published in 1966. Both
books analyse the systems of representation which, as Barthes says
in the Foreword, structure not just specific phenomena but also
the 'image system of our time', even the very notion of rationality
itself (*Fashion*, xi). Humans are caught 'Between Things and
Words' (the title of Chapter 3 of *The Fashion System* echoes the
French title of *The Order of Things*, *Les mots et les choses*). They are
transfixed by a system which codes their perceptions, institu-
tionalises creativity, and organises reality itself. So the book shut-
tles between the apocalyptic and the crashing mundanity of
fashion writing, sometimes managing the transition with irony,
sometimes falling heavily into bleak abstraction.

Like Foucault's look at the natural historians of the eighteenth
and nineteenth centuries in *The Order of Things*, Barthes is fascinated by the classifications, the 'species' and 'genera' (his terms) of
the fashion magazines, which he tries to net with the meshes of
structuralist semiology. But the gaps between the analytic dryness
and the denunciatory rhetoric make the book brittle. Barthes stares
at a pulverised meaning system empty of human agency: 'it is the

sequence of constraints, and not that of freedoms, which best describes this structure' (*Fashion*, 161). The fashion system is one of the earliest of postmodern consumer wastelands: a world of manufactured, inauthentic desire endlessly recycling itself without memory or purpose. Often dismissed as unreadably dull (because tracts of it are), *The Fashion System* is Barthes's most violent denunciation of the circuitry of exploitative consumerism; it also contains a neo-Sartrean account of vitiated selves, poor beyond imagining, whose desires are fed by corrupted meanings, and in whose thin memories duration is abolished, 'reduced to the couple of what is driven out and what is inaugurated'. Fashion is 'an amnesiac substitution of the present for the past' (*Fashion*, 289).[7]

The Fashion System is Barthes's bleakest book, both stylistically and thematically. Though it seems sometimes to yearn towards its opposite, the 'hot' Barthes occasionally glimpsed in the practised selection of comic examples, its mode of argument falls easily into line with his most chilly scenarios of inevitable alienation. In *The Fashion System* these have an added dimension. The opposition between the systems of inert convention and the 'poetic zone' of literature hardens into a tacit opposition of 'the literary' to 'the mass' which Barthes explored with greater vigour after his 'structuralist period'. However, Barthes's attitudes to popular creativity were not always so negative, nor was his use of the analytic tackle of structuralism so demolishing. In the next two sections of this chapter we will look first at some different ways of using structuralist thinking, then compare Barthes's work on popular culture with that of significant comtemporaries.

Applications

Barthes's most influential structuralist work was not the theoretical toolbox of *Elements*, nor the consumer jeremiad of *The Fashion System*. For a variety of reasons (not least the conceptual and verbal abstraction of these books) it is the more directly engaged essays collected in *Mythologies* (1957) which have had more lasting impact. This section will therefore begin with a look at this book and its legacy before moving to a consideration of Barthes's important, related essay 'Introduction to the structural analysis of narratives' (1966).

Mythologies, perhaps Barthes's best-known volume, consists mainly of brief, witty essays originally written as journalism between 1952 and 1956 and signed R.B. in ironic homage to B.B., Brigitte Bardot, the leading European sex symbol of the era. The subject matter is diverse, but the collection is probably best seen as a sardonic panorama of French culture during a period of crucial change, particularly the dramatic shift towards consumer-orientated 'modernisation' which had parallels across Western Europe during the postwar boom. Once again, therefore, structuralist analysis is deployed in relation to popular culture, but unlike *The Fashion System*, and despite initial complaints of jargon and difficulty, most of these essays read easily, with a deft comic touch which has been widely imitated in Britain.[8] Barthes's biographer suggests that in France *Mythologies* influenced not just journalists and critics, but novelists and the film-makers of the 'New Wave', especially Godard; while, like Marshall McLuhan's work in the States, Barthes's analyses of consumerism were not lost on the advertising industry itself, ironically one of the book's main targets.[9]

It is impossible to divorce the originality of *Mythologies* from its context, and the book should be seen in relation not just to the theoretical abstractions of high structuralism (which it preceded) but also to the 'thematic' analyses of *Michelet*, and the essays collected in *Critical Essays* (1963), with which it overlapped. In an interview from 1962, Barthes described himself as primarily an essayist (*Grain*, 8); and Michel Foucault thought Barthes's essays one of the period's most powerful intellectual and polemical interventions.[10] So the *Mythologies* pieces, in their brevity, punch and search for a wider audience, should be seen as attempts to address an 'engaged' situation, and it is essential not to sacrifice this topicality to an overriding concern with method. Looked at as a whole – the best-known of the English translations prints just over half of the original – *Mythologies* participates in many of the urgent debates which preoccupied Left intellectuals across Europe. These include questions of imperial withdrawal, the increasing influence of American cultural forms and habits, the development of technocratic models and icons, the cultural 'condition' of a consumerist working class becoming increasingly (it was claimed) more petit bourgeois (a favourite term of abuse for Barthes), and the complacent response of institutional authority to these changes. Some of these issues will be addressed comparatively in the next section, but first we need a sense of their range across *Mythologies* itself.

Barthes's 1957 Preface is very lucid about his intentions. The essays were written out of resentment that 'Nature and History [are] confused at every turn, and I wanted to track down, in the decorative display of *what-goes-without-saying*, that ideological abuse which, in my view, is hidden there' (*Myth*, 11) His enemy, therefore – like Jimmy Porter's in John Osborne's coeval *Look Back in Anger* (1956) – is the 'falsely obvious', the mendacity of a complacent, dishonest culture which conceals actual history beneath the pretence that all is well and all is natural. The *Mythologies*, therefore, are largely topical – recent news items and journalistic features, new exhibitions, films or books, advertisements for detergents, cars or beauty products, everyday habits, and so on. All these form the 'mythological' façade of a culture whose outline is familiar from Barthes's earlier work. Beneath the often-comical sparkle of the surface of *Mythologies* lie the stark lineaments of the detested totality. Thus Barthes sarcastically admits his lack of 'objectivity' and embittered repetitiveness, but he asserts with gusto his existential authenticity among all this lying: 'what I claim is to live to the full the contradiction of my time, which may well make sarcasm the condition of truth' (*Myth*, 12).

The *Mythologies* are not academic in any traditional sense. They rely on a quick eye, wit, surprise and impertinent comparison (wrestling matches are like Racine or Molière; the names of plastics – polystyrene, polyvinyl – are like pastoral shepherds). Their only predecessor, as far as I know, is Marshall McLuhan's neglected early volume *The Mechanical Bride* (1951), which tours American popular publications exposing the mechanisms of consumer passivication and the ominous 'condition of public helplessness' they produce with the same mixture of wit and invective.[11] Barthes's essays, too, often have a homiletic shape ending in a noisy political lesson. The consistent argument – the structuralist argument – is that objects and events signify more than themselves. They are caught in systems of representation which 'add' meaning to existence (a diet of steak, chips and wine, for instance, signifies a representative 'Frenchness').

These systems are mythic in two senses: in the common sense, they are false meanings and are designed to deceive; but more importantly, these myths are public systems like religions, and demand collective assent. They organise the assumptions and beliefs which bond a culture together. Indeed, a trail of substitutions and displacements for religion in popular practices and products runs through *Mythologies*: the new Citroën (model name, the 'Goddess') is like a Gothic cathederal; the spiritual and the show-business worlds overlap in Billy Graham's evangelism or 'The iconography of the Abbé Pierre' (a Catholic priest who worked with the homeless in the bitter Paris winters); aviators are saints and test pilots are monastic in the essay 'The jet-man'; and in *The Lost Continent*, Barthes analyses the modern Church's bland absorption of the world's religions into a vague, universal humanitarianism. In *The Lost Continent* – a documentary film about the Orient which, according to Barthes, peddles Western myths about exotic innocence – the rites, folklore and ceremonies of local people 'are never related to a particular historical order, an explicit economic or social status, but only the great neutral forms of cosmic commonplaces' (*Myth*, 95). The effect is to universalise Western prejudices. For whom, asks Barthes, is this continent 'lost' at a time of French (and British) imperial withdrawal?

Barthes's myths, therefore, are very different from those of poets like Robert Graves or Ted Hughes in Britain in the same period. For these writers, as we have seen, mythology was a personal existential schema against which the writer tested his authenticity. For Barthes, on the contrary, mythology is not personal but social. It is a structural condition like 'Literature'. *Mythologies*, therefore, is concerned to reveal – in Barthes's characteristic, long-term project – the modes of 'intelligibility of the age', how his own period chooses to understand itself (*Grain*, 8). He wishes to establish the 'thematics' of contemporary life, and links with *Michelet*, then being written, are clear throughout in, for instance, the use made of bodily processes. Like Michelet, Barthes himself often judges by sensual pleasure or repulsion, and in *Mythologies* he detests the clammy, viscid myths that metaphorically coat reality.

The connection is also evident in the contradictory exuberance of Barthes's response to many of the new myths he claims to detest. As in *Michelet*, the ostensible object of his disapproval can inspire excited reactions. Towards the close of *Mythologies* he writes of the pain of 'the evaporation of reality' in myth, but of how, therefore, 'I have started to make it excessively dense, and to discover in it a surprising compactness which I savoured with delight' (*Myth*, 158). This divided response is widely apparent. In 'Two myths of the new theatre', for instance, he writes of a new play in which 'the two male partners spread themselves in liquids of all kinds, tears, sweat and saliva. It is as if we were watching a dreadful psychological labour, a monstrous torsion of the internal tissues, as if passion were a huge wet sponge squeezed by the playwright's implacable hand' (*Eiffel*, 75). Barthes hated overly realistic acting which pretended to be 'just like life', and favoured austere stylised forms. But in the horrible secreting monster portrayed here there is an ambiguous Keatsian relish for the physicality of the image which creates a paradoxical, but very Barthesian, effect. The language itself pushes in a direction contrary to the explicit sense.

Mythologies surveys a number of key aspects of French life in the 1950s. Among these are a fascinated analysis of consumer invention, balanced by an equal hostilty to its mind-snatching mythological prowess. Like Sartre, Barthes hated the complacency of the French national mood in the 1950s epitomised by self-congratulatory television and the mystique of the technology of affluence: jets, cars and domestic gadgets.[12] The antiquated, but none the less adaptive, national institutions were (as in Britain in the same period) a particular target, and *Mythologies* contains attacks on the intellectual and moral atrophy of the judicial system in 'Dominici, or the triumph of literature' and 'The Dupriez trial' which anticipate Foucault's more famous and sustained analyses in the 1970s. The book also makes fun of conventional domestic rituals and marriage, and attacks, in a strikingly sympathetic way for the period, the mythic representations of women in the home in 'Novels and children' and, especially, 'Agony columns'. But the most sustained political topic in *Mythologies* concerns imperialism and, in particular, the French involvements in Indo-China and Algeria, where a lengthy terrorist war was being fought which eventually led to independence in 1962. The Algerian events played a major part in the French domestic crisis leading to the creation of de Gaulle's Fifth Republic in 1958.

Barthes's attention to the Algerian situation, and imperialism generally, is very insistent throughout *Mythologies*, and several splendid essays – like 'African grammar' and 'Bichon and the Blacks' (both in *The Eiffel Tower*) – are devoted to these questions.

But Barthes's concern is, as it were, structural rather than issue-specific. He is interested in the way French culture blocks out reference to its own difficulties and constructs an alternative dimension of meaning to sustain other economic and political imperatives. Thus in an essay on wine he reminds his audience that the production of the French 'national' drink is imposed on teetotal, dispossessed Muslims in Algeria who lack bread: 'it is typical of our current alienation' that wine 'cannot be an unalloyed blissful substance, except if we wrongly forget that it is also the product of an expropriation' (*Myth*, 61). Barthes objects not to the pleasures of wine (unlike many on the Left, he was always an enthusiast for pleasure) but to the convenient forgetting which sustains consumption-driven myths about the world.

This is an issue which has grown much more important subsequently, as Western writers have become more conscious of their international situation (a similar point to Barthes's is made by Seamus Heaney in his poem 'Oysters' in *Field Work* [1979] for instance), but it was rarely raised in the 1950s. In his autobiography *Unreasonable Behaviour*, the war photographer Don Mc-Cullin, whose career can be seen as a tour around the global crises of postwar decolonisation, describes the reflex patriotic Eurocentrism of a period in which independence fighters like the Mau–Mau in Kenya (where McCullin served as a National Serviceman) were seen as 'monster baddie Indians, well-known from the blood-curdling tales in the Other Ranks' Mess of atrocities and unspeakable oath-taking ceremonies'.[13] McCullin's remark neatly illustrates the blend of gut patriotism and popular Hollywood mythology typical of the period. So one of Barthes's intentions in addressing what are now (controversially) called 'Third World' issues is that the radical otherness of life in Western Europe's colonial backyard reveals the untruths of the cosy myths fostered by ignorance and interests at home. This point is widely tackled in *Mythologies*: for instance, in the several essays on tourism, or that on the well-intentioned, American-inspired photographic exhibition 'The Great Family of Man', which pretends to view the world with the benign superior neutrality of God, all of whose children are ostensibly already equal (*Myth*, 100–2).

The process outlined here is the basic revelation of Barthes's structural model in *Mythologies*. Myths are based on a concealment of some meanings and the interested promotion of others: wine is good; the facts of Algerian wine production remain a secret. In one essay, 'The Romans in films', Barthes calls for an 'ethic of signs'. All signs, he remarks, are actually only 'surface' features, simple, partial indications. But myths try to pass themselves off as 'depth' or truth, possessing the substance of reality itself. Barthes therefore prefers signs which flaunt themselves as such – for example, the stylised acting techniques of Japanese or classical Greek theatre, or the flagrant histrionics of commercial wrestling. These signs avoid the corrupting duplicities of mythic speech. Everybody knows where they are in such systems. *Mythologies* therefore closes with a much longer and justly celebrated essay, 'Myth today', which draws together the methodological principles developed through his more instinctive journalism. 'Myth today' is the point where Barthes's structuralism and the 'thematic' methods of *Michelet* come together. In the terms we have been using to designate the polarities of his writing, 'Myth today' is the 'cool' rationalisation of the 'hot' flurry of Barthes's monthly columns in *Lettres Nouvelles*.

'Myth today' deploys the Saussurean model more fully developed in *Elements of Semiology* and *The Fashion System*, though it is doubtful whether these later books take it much further in useful practice. For the model, in itself, is helpfully simple, and 'Myth today' has, throughout, a lucid elegance that is not always characteristic of semiological writing. At its heart, Barthes posits a 'pyramidal' process based on Saussure's division of the sign into signifier (the vocal or graphic mark) and signified (the mental concept attached to it). The relation between these two, it will be remembered, is arbitrary – that is, conventional. In the analysis of written myth, Barthes calls these signs a '*first-order*' signifying system. 'Mythic' speech, however, takes the process a stage further. It takes already-established first-order signs, and from them develops a '*second-order semiological system*' (*Myth*, 114). For example, the word 'rose' is the sign in English by which we designate a certain common English garden plant, and especially its flower (this is the 'referent' in linguistic parlance). But the sign 'rose' has multiple associations which are gathered over time and enable the sign 'rose' to function symbolically. In Barthes's own example, when one gives one's loved one a rose, the flower signifies one's passion; it is a kind of mythic or symbolic representation of love. It is then open to poets (for instance) to exploit this mythology of the sign 'rose', as in Burns and countless Valentine's cards:

O, my Luve's like a red, red rose
That's newly sprung in June;

This is a simple example of 'mythic speech', a 'poetic' appropriation of a sign for purposes of sentiment. In Burns, the mythic sign 'rose' makes itself obvious (it is a formal simile used with self-conscious conventionality), but in other discourses the associations of roses are used for commerce (chocolates, for instance) or for politics (the Labour Party); or for the iconography of sport, religion, the northern counties, England itself, regiments of the army, a dream of rural housing – indeed, it sometimes seems impossible to look at the plant itself without engaging a cultural matrix. But despite the prolixity of the mythic associations of roses, the basic structuralist point holds: that a rose by any other name would still be in a signifying system. One cannot transcend the cultural structure in which all signification must be embedded.

These 'second-order' systems, then, proliferate beyond the innocence of the 'first-order' system. Indeed, Barthes argues, it is the apparent naturalness or innocence of the 'first-order' system which anchors the authenticity of myth. We all know that roses are beautiful and so are lovers, but we usually forget that roses have greenfly and thorns. Similarly, *Mythologies* is full of examples of a world transformed by the mendacious, interested magic of 1950s consumerism, and it is easy to match this from present experience of an evening's television or 'lifestyle' advertising. In recent advertisements for Coca-Cola, for instance, the drink is relentlessly associated with stylish, healthy leisure to the point where a bond is made between the signifier 'Coke' and the signified 'youthful, stylish, affluent, healthy leisure', which is mythic. In such advertisements the rapid layers of 'first-order' signs engage each other at such a rate, and with such repetition, that their networks of association 'cover' reality with sticky myth. As the managing director of Coca-Cola UK recently put it in *The Times:* 'We're not just a brown fizzy drink, you know. We're a way of life.' For 'way of life' he might have said 'myth' in Barthes's sense.

Modern advertising is a spectacular example of Barthesian myth-making. But to enable further work, it is important to understand the method of analysis of the structural transformations which occur in such processes. Myths capitalise the conventional 'arbitrariness' of the sign's relationships, and cash in its multiple networks of association. In this process the original meaning (let alone the referent) is sometimes left behind. Recently, highly successful advertisements for a make of German car ran the slogan 'Vorsprung durch Technik', which literally means 'staying ahead with technology'. But only a tiny fraction of those at whom the advertisements were aimed would understand the literal sense, which was never explained. Instead, the slogan capitalised on a certain mythic 'Germanness' carrying very positive associations in this context: technological efficiency and innovation, reliability, manufacturing thoroughness, sophisticated Europeanness, and so on. The point is that myth structurally uproots 'first-order' language, selecting from its diverse meanings by promoting some while silencing others. The significatory resources of language are thereby restricted, and myth distorts our response to the world by ruthless and narrow selection. For Barthes, this has two consequences.

First, mythic speech misrepresents the world according to certain interests, because we assume that language is a natural instrument of 'truthful' representation. This is why Barthes prefers signs which frankly reveal themselves as such. But secondly, Barthes opposes mythic speech because it narrows language's signifying potential, and thereby reduces the human capacity for creative usage. Instead of being a playful, creative joy, mythic language is shackled to meagre interests. As we shall see in Chapter 3, it was this second argument which eventually became, for Barthes, the more important. But in *Mythologies* itself it is the first argument which is dominant, because it has the most immediate relationship to the political context. The structural analysis of myth is necessary, he argues in 'Myth today', because of the 'development of publicity, of a national press, of radio, of illustrated news, not to speak of the survival of a myriad rites of communication which rule social appearances. . . . In a single day, how many really nonsignifying fields do we cross?' (*Myth*, 112). Here Barthes is picturing a fallen world of language, full of rites and power, which none the less desires to pass itself off as innocently natural. As in *The Fashion System*, there is no world beyond that already signified in appearances. As in *Writing Degree Zero*, the argument must imply a role for the writer as an enemy of orthodoxy. 'At bottom,' writes Barthes, 'it would only be the zero degree which could resist myth' (*Myth*, 132) – because myth, like a virus, invades the stuff of language itself, and performs the ideological distortion of reality.

Thus the imagery Barthes uses to describe mythic language in 'Myth today' repeats the political targets of the essays: it is spuriously religious, 'robbery by colonization' (*Myth*, 132), and has the sloppiness of advertising slogans: 'the knowledge contaminated in a mythical concept is confused, made of yielding, shapeless associations . . . a formless, unstable, nebulous condensation whose unity and coherence are above all due to its function' (*Myth*, 119). It is in passages like this that 'Myth today' comes closest to *Michelet* and a somewhat conventional, humanitarian protest against a radically alienated world. It shapes a rhetoric of mythic deluge, a flowing, shapeless liquidity which 'steeps', 'wallows', 'haemorrhages' across the culture, bathing its victims in its 'sickness', 'contamination' and 'nausea'.

This language is reminiscent of *Michelet*, but the scenario is the ghastly environment of the dehumanised undead sketched in *Writing Degree Zero* and *The Fashion System*. It is a global village in which everyone has been bitten by the vampires of myth. Barthes speaks of how, in mythic language, 'the meaning loses its value but keeps its life' (*Myth*, 118); of how authentic history is evaporated, but a whole new history is 'implanted' (*Myth*, 119). The rhetorical scenario has its basis in horror or sci-fi films or fiction in which the hero awakes to find his neighbours enslaved by a slithery substance or invader. (It is the scenario of vampire films, *The Invasion of the Body Snatchers*, *The Day of the Triffids*, and countless other productions of the period.) In *Mythologies* this, once again, creates a curious instability in which a 'hot' rhetoric of protest contradicts the depressive clarity of the diagnosis of an incurably sick culture in which the human world seems forever on the verge of blurring into the world of things. Humans are continually portrayed as passive victims or willing consumer-dupes. For the brave analyst-hero, it seems, the only prospects are to become reified himself, as the remote essence of language in the lonely resistance of the zero degree; or, with collusive savour, to indulge with relish the inner organs of myth and structure.

Often treated as a methodological model, *Mythologies* is better read as a methodological elaboration which emerges from a reactive immersion in a cultural situation. But within this, and given Barthes's bleak reading of the cultural direction of his period, it is easy to see the possibilities sketched in 'Myth today'. The analytic model of 'first- and second-order systems' has several advantages for the analysis of complex signifying systems. It is able to describe them with a clear-headed structural lucidity, but also to close the gap between formal description and ideological and social content. But most importantly, the model can accommodate different kinds of phenomena, and in 1966 Barthes turned his structuralism to narrative analysis in one of his best-known essays, 'Introduction to the structural analysis of narratives'. Originally intended – rather in the manner of *Elements of Semiology* – as a primer on the subject, it starts from the view that narrative is a universal activity, and tries to identify the essential structural features of storytelling. The model he adopts is the one theorised in 'Myth today' – that is, the 'pyramidal' model whereby the significance of one element is capitalised at the level above. The significance of roses, thus, is given by the mythology of love into which it is integrated. The same principle holds for the analysis of narrative. What is significant in a narrative is what is picked up and developed later. What is most significant is what travels furthest through the narrative and plays a part in its resolution. Barthes uses the detective story as an example. Detective stories scatter information very carefully, teasing the reader to recognise the clue which will lead to the identification of the criminal. One by one these clues are discarded, and only one strand persists, leading to the revelation. The same principle remains true at all levels. What is most significant about a character, for instance, will be that which is repeated, not a stray detail of dress or appearance.

The essay develops a series of sometimes unhelpful terms derived from Barthes's reading in linguistics to describe the various strata at which the narrative operates. The main components of the structural analysis of narratives are *actions*, *sequences* (or *syntax*), and *functions* (or *indices*). *Actions* are the building blocks of narrative, and Barthes's theory holds good here: a significant action is one which leads to another in sequence to form the *syntax* of the narrative's organisation. In the mini-narrative 'While the boy threw the ball to the dog, she set the fuse which she carried to the van and blew up the park', the first action (throwing the ball) is much less important, because it does not directly integrate with the second (setting the fuse), which integrates with the third and concluding action (*boom!*). You could dispense with the boy and his ball, and the narrative would survive. This does not mean to say that the boy is insignificant (effect is added through the vulnerable detail), but Barthes is keen to see action, not character, as the keystone of narrative. The boy and the ball in Barthes's terms are *functions* or *indices*. Essentially, *functions* distribute material around the path of the narrative: the false clue, the point of ambiguity or connection (might the boy in the narrative above be in fact a decoy?). *Indices*, on the other hand, draw material together like the description of atmosphere, location, character, or even the writer's 'philosophy'. But *indices* are dispensable; if a description of atmosphere were omitted, the narrative might be the poorer, but it would survive.

Barthes's narrative structuralism, then, is descriptively interesting. It can contribute to a significant knowledge of formal organisation in narrative by providing both terminology and working principles. But what is striking about it is, first, that it works most clearly on simple narratives, and, second, that it leaves out or downgrades many of the features of narratives to which readers respond most enthusiastically: the semantic level (what does this narrative mean?) and the level of character or psychology. For Barthes, though, there are good reasons for this. For him, as for Aristotle, action in narrative is more important than character, and there is an obvious way in which this is true. Most narratives consumed in the world are in fact based not on psychology but on stereotype: this is true of folk tales, ballads, soap operas, romances, detective stories, science fiction, and most television. The names and details change, but the roles and functions remain. For Barthes, therefore, what is commonly called psychology or character in fiction is no such thing; it is a myth which should be analysed not on the level of behaviour, but on that of its narrative or mythic function. The same is true of the semantic level, which Barthes also tends to relegate to mythic analysis. What a writer has to say about the world is of much less importance than the structural function of it: what myths does it feed or embrace, what components of the system does it redistribute?

'Introduction to the structural analysis of narratives' displays all the strengths and weaknesses of Barthes's structuralism. Its strengths lie in its analytic rigour and the thoughtful terminology it provides to discuss aspects of form which are often merely matters of impression. The weaknesses are equally evident. This structuralism downgrades content and the semantic level, and while this is not so important in, say, the detective story, it would be a stubbornly blunt-headed formalist who would think that *King Lear*, *Middlemarch* or *A la recherche du temps perdu* had nothing to say beyond the organisation of their parts. So in a way there is a kind of remoteness in structuralist analysis which refuses to open dialogues of meaning with other work; and this is perhaps why, in the work of Barthes and others, structuralism confines itself so closely to commercial culture. Most of the examples in the essay on narratives are drawn from the James Bond novel *Goldfinger*, and we shall see in Chapter 3 what happens when Barthes starts to work on semantically more complex narrative material. In the end, perhaps, structuralism's greatest difficulty lies in coming to terms with own lack of analytic suppleness.

Parallels

Structuralist methodology had a number of advantages for Barthes. Analysing commercial culture produced for the market, structuralism is able to account for the systematic production of meaning in a way which is more difficult for traditional literary criticism committed to the unique text or writer. Barthes conducts a series of analyses from the individual advertisement or behaviour, through the mythic system, to the economic and ideological structures which hold the ensemble in place. His analysis of mythology, therefore, is of a piece with other forms of socially inclined structuralism by, for example, Foucault, Lévi-Strauss or Althusser, in a period which encouraged many fears across the West that an increasingly superficial and homogenised culture was growing unchecked.

But structuralism's commitment to system rather than the individual event produces a tension within *Mythologies*. The excitement of innovative methods and new materials contradicts the gloomy general scenarios of determinism and limitation. Structuralism, it seems, offers an intellectually complex mode of understanding for phenomena which the analysis itself reveals, in the end, to be simple and routinised. The top-heavy effect, as is commonly remarked, emphasises the estrangement between the intellectual and common life. Two related objections, therefore, to Barthes's structuralism are, first, that it condescendingly portrays 'the mass' as unconscious, passive victims; and, second, that because of its commitment to system, structuralism is unresponsive to the complexity of individual texts or persons. Both objections have considerable force, and are particularly pertinent to the political dimension of *Mythologies*.

Barthes himself had considerable distaste for political activism, and never involved himself in it. In 1960, despite his opposition to government policy, he refused to sign the 'manifeste des 121', a petition organised by leading intellectuals against the Algerian War. This reluctance was partly temperamental, but also a rationalisation to the effect that all political discourses sooner or later reinstate the structures of power they intend to oppose. Barthes's politics, therefore, are disengaged in a way which has been attacked.[14] His sceptical pessimism produces the descriptions of monolithic authority which pervade his work, and the view that worthwhile intellectuals and writers are inevitably alienated beings. In *The Fashion System* he argues that all sign systems, once they enter the world, are 'filled' by it, and hence alienated from themselves. Therefore, 'in order to comprehend the world, it [the system of signs] must withdraw from it; a profound antinomy separates the model for productive behaviour and that for reflexive behaviour, systems of actions and systems of meanings' (*Fashion*, 290). Interestingly, Barthes chooses to assign choice to systems, not to people.

Barthes's position is similar to that of others on the French Left in the period. His idea that myth 'buttonholes' individuals, and constructs an approved self-image to which they haplessly aspire, is one of the most suggestive passages of political analysis in *Mythologies*, and anticipates Althusser's better-known account of the process which both called 'interpellation' (*Myth*, 124–5, 148).[15] Similarly, Barthes's characterisation of a uniform society imposing its ideological mind-set on a gawping multitude is paralleled in 'Situationist' theory, in which capitalist-consumer society is imaged as an hypnotic spectacle.[16] But these models were opposed. In France, Sartre and, especially, Henri Lefebvre had long had an interest in the 'politics of everyday life', and both angrily argued that the structuralist model was actually complicit with capitalist alienation and bureaucratic rationality.[17] In Britain, similar arguments were made by the historian E.P. Thompson in *The Poverty of Theory* (1978). Thompson charged Althusser particularly with having a shrivelled sense of historical processes, and neglecting the significance of human agency and creativity. For Thompson the structuralist reading of culture as totalised alienation neglected and devalued the powerful dissident tradition, and thereby disabled the very opposition to capitalist authority in whose name structuralist analysis was conducted.

For all his polemical foibles, Thompson makes a compelling case, because structuralism has serious difficulties in this respect. At the close of *Mythologies*, Barthes becomes entangled in the contradiction that he simultaneously supports dissent and regards it as futile. His alienated mythologist is 'excluded from this history in the name of which he professes to act', and a better future is unimaginable, because 'tomorrow's positivity is entirely hidden by today's negativity . . . the most potent seed of the future *is nothing but* the most profound apocalypse of the present' (*Myth*, 157). His flight from culture refuses to recognise any existing human behaviour which might bring a better future into being. In this context a revealing contrast might be made with contemporary work by Raymond Williams in Britain. Williams was a critic of the same generation as Barthes. He, too, saw literature in social terms, and was interested in the relations between art and popular communications. Like Barthes's, his work began as a response to the specific political and cultural changes of the postwar period, but his attitudes to these – also from the Left – are strikingly different.

Williams's essay 'Culture is ordinary' (1958) begins with the writer waiting for a bus (already an unlikely Barthesian venue) and conducts a tour through cultural locations representative of contemporary attitudes. The opening paragraph juxtaposes a cathedral's locked library, which Williams has just visited, with the local cinema, which is showing *Six-Five Special*. The contrast, as always with Williams, emphasises the borderlands: the difference between locked and accessible cultures, between the popular and the minority (the library books are in Latin), between different forms of education and access, between different levels of power and authority. But for Williams, culture is found in these interacting tensions, which are diverse, both rich *and* ordinary, exclusive *and* inclusive: 'The making of a society is the finding of common meanings and directions, and its growth is an active debate and amendment under the pressures of experience, contact, and discovery.'[18] Though Williams, too, attacks advertising (the 'new cheapjack in offices with contemporary *décor*, using scraps of linguistics, psychology and sociology to influence what he thinks of as the mass mind': Williams, 7) and the 'fixed and partial' attitudes of the cultural establishment, the model of fluid growth and common movement (on the bus) is strikingly different from the stasis and apocalyptic haemorrhages of *Mythologies*. For Williams, culture is 'always both traditional and creative' (Williams, 4); and it is that 'both' which is crucial and different.

Williams attacks the habit of speaking of the 'ignorant masses'. It is simply untrue, he argues, to characterise a complex culture in the rigid generalities of either the establishment or its opposition. In a comment pertinent to Barthes's limited political vocabulary, Williams remarks that 'a great part of the English way of life, and of its arts and learning, is not bourgeois in any discoverable sense' (Williams, 8). Terms like 'mass', 'bourgeois', 'a dying culture', and the like, are projections, not observations, and Williams refuses to condemn consumer products as mere myths: 'I will not listen with patience to any acid listing of them – you know the sneer you can get into plumbing, baby Austins, aspirin, contraceptives, canned food. But I say to these Pharisees: dirty water, an earth bucket, a four-mile walk to work, headaches, broken women, hunger and monotony of diet' (Williams, 10). So there are real difficulties in Barthes's social designations and descriptions. Towards the close of 'Culture is ordinary', Williams has a passage on the 'new dissenters' who have soured 'the democratic idea' by 'the apparent division of our culture into, on the one hand, a remote and self-gracious sophistication, on the other hand a doped mass'. The result is 'angry self-exile' (Williams, 17). Of course he did not have Barthes in mind, but he might have done.

There are, of course, difficulties with Williams's model too, but the contrast between it and Barthes's work is revealing.[19] At the close of *Mythologies*, Barthes writes:

> the speech of the oppressed can only be poor, monotonous and immediate: his destitution is the very yardstick of his language: he has only one, always the same, that of his actions; metalanguage is a luxury, he cannot have access to it. . . . This essential barrenness produces rare threadbare myths: either transient or clumsily indiscreet. (*Myth*, 148)

In other words, non-bourgeois language does not even have the luxury of self-corrupting myths. The poor, the proletariat, the oppressed (Barthes's vocabulary is used undiscriminatingly) are unable to initiate or develop. It is an extraordinarily condescending portrait for a thinker on the Left, and one which has been attacked by one French critic, Michel Ragon, as 'cultural genocide'.[20]

This habit of Barthes's persisted. In a later essay, 'Pax culturalis' (1971), first published in the *Times Literary Supplement*, Barthes claims that 'the proletariat (the producers) has no culture of its own' (*Rustle*, 103). It is therefore forced into crass repetitions of inert 'bourgeois' forms. Indeed, Barthes argues, positive culture is an illusion 'like an imperishable corpse: it is a bizarre toy that *History never breaks*' (*Rustle*, 100). Culture does not offer possibilities. Its function is the enforcement of inertia, the preservation of the same banality that has ruled from Balzac to the American television serial. In culture there is only the commonplace. There is no playful disruption:

> The result is that this succession not only separates men from each other, but each man, each individual is in himself lacerated; each day in myself, there accumulate, without communicating, several isolated languages: I am fragmented, isolated, scattered (which in other circumstances passes for the very definition of 'madness').
> (*Rustle*, 102)

This nightmare of psychologically butchered isolation is Barthes's most negative critical mood, but it is one which is closely tied to a discreditable social analysis and conclusion. Barthes never came to terms with the difference between popular and commercial culture, and between what people receive and how they respond. He never recognised the existence of uncanonical writing, or forms of oral or behaviourally based culture.

In this he is not exceptional. Such confusions are endemic to a rapid step from textual analysis to cultural generalisation. Indeed, Pierre Bourdieu argued impressively in his book *La Distinction* (1979) that French cultural analysis generally has been vitiated by the inappropriate assumptions of a persistent aristocratic model 'personified by a Parisian *haute bourgeoisie* which, combining all forms of prestige and all titles of economic and social mobility, has no counterpart elsewhere, at least in the arrogance of its cultural judgements'.[21] While Barthes was no natural member of this elite, it is true that his work can show the same lordly disdain, and in reading *Mythologies* it is hard not to be conscious that alongside its virtues the book is, in one sense at least (as Bourdieu says of the whole tradition), 'legitimating social differences' through its encouragement of class stereotypes and valuations.

Barthes's remoteness from immediate politics goes hand in hand with an individualism which he cultivated increasingly as his career progressed, and which is in some fundamental respects at odds with his early commitment to the Left. For him valuable writing is always achieved on the run from 'Literature', and *Mythologies* offers an 'ethic of signs' based not on politics but on a somewhat naive significatory honesty which allows individuals to make clear assessments of social situations. Like many controversial dissidents whose values are primarily personal (D.H. Lawrence comes to mind as an example in Britain), Barthes conceives of society itself as inevitably injurious to individual integrity. In his final interview he remarked: 'I now believe that the only truly consistent marginalism is individualism' (*Grain*, 363); and during his final decade he developed value systems based on an increasingly explicit nihilism: 'I believe that nihilism is the only possible philosophy for our current situation. But . . . I do not confuse nihilism with violent, radically destructive behaviour, or . . . with behaviour that is more or less neurotic or hysterical' (*Grain*, 155). This remark is interesting because it is so evasive.

A defence which Barthes himself made from time to time was that he defines politics differently. He is interested not in sociality but in the politics of the imagination. In collective myth the producer and the consumer, the dominant and the passive, the ruler and the ruled, merge together, stifling individual desire and imagination. Barthes analyses several unhealthy consequences of this in *The Fashion System* – for example, the loss of memory which occurs in a system geared only to novelty (*Fashion*, 289), or the elimination of choice in the ethereal fiats and proverbs of fashion (*Fashion*, 271). The bizarre contrast of the unworldly language of advertising and thoroughly worldly retailing, Barthes shrewdly argues, reflects the paradox of the fashion system itself: 'Fashion must project the aristocratic model, the source of its prestige . . . but at the same time it must represent, in a euphoric manner, the world of its consumers by transforming intra-worldly functions into signs (work, sport, vacations, seasons, ceremonies)' (*Fashion*, 290–1). It is, he argues, both a 'luxurious spectacle' (implying the choice to watch or not) and a 'program of behaviour' (*Fashion*,

291). In these ways Barthes perhaps does put urgent questions to his immediate period, and confronts the problem raised by Bourdieu. For Barthes, it is not the analysis which is aristocratic, but the political engineering of modern consumerism.

Barthes's work on popular culture is part of a widespread interest in the subject throughout the West in the 1950s, and it is helpful to see *Mythologies* and *The Fashion System* in relation to arguments which go beyond structuralism. The *locus classicus* for discussion of popular culture in Britain at this time was probably Richard Hoggart's *The Uses of Literacy* which appeared, as an exact contemporary of *Mythologies*, in 1957. Like *Mythologies*, *The Uses of Literacy* is, in its own way, an innovative book, mixing autobiography, literary criticism and a densely immediate attention to Northern working-class experience which is rich with Hoggart's intelligent familiarity (he came from this background himself). In France, *The Uses of Literacy* was received with the shock of the new. The introduction to the French edition could find no place for it in the traditions of European anthropology or the sociology of class. If anything, wrote Jean-Claude Passeron, *The Uses of Literacy* was like the ethnography produced by visitors to far-flung tribes, though with an important difference: Hoggart was no visitor. Hoggart's language, Passeron argues, was uniquely able to disclose the essence of working-class life. It exactly mirrored the forms of this experience itself. As a result, Hoggart bypasses the elitism of most academic analyses of the working class, and mounts a critique of many political intellectuals' relations with the social group for whom they claimed to speak.[22] On this account, *The Uses of Literacy* is a kind of alter ego to Barthes's work, and a comparison will bring out some of the reasons why *Mythologies* became so influential.

There is, of course, some truth to Passeron's argument, and it is easy now to lose sight of the originality of *The Uses of Literacy*. But in other respects his claims are more contentious. We might first note how different is his attitude to language. For him (and there is warrant for his argument in *The Uses of Literacy* itself), Hoggart's language is radically realist: it reflects, as Passeron puts it, 'the structures, if not always the words, of working-class consciousness and speech' (Passeron, 124). Structuralists, however, argue that language is fundamentally systematic and conventional. It is an anti-realist view, especially in Barthes's hands. The two attitudes to language represented by Barthes and Hoggart have been fundamentally opposed in recent years, and it is certainly a major problem for structuralism that language seems to be so independent of human control. For Barthes, in his 'high'-structuralist phase, language sometimes seems so theoretically alien that one wonders how he can use it himself with such delicacy. Nowadays, it is unlikely that many would make the exorbitant claims made in, say, *The Fashion System*, but it is worth recalling why such arguments did seem persuasive.

Passeron argues that the language of *The Uses of Literacy* is at one with its subject because of Hoggart's intimate experience, and because the book bypasses mainstream ways of writing about the subject. But, in fact, even if this is true within sociology, Passeron fails to recognise the very Anglo–Saxon tradition of literary analysis and personal sociological witness on which *The Uses of Literacy* draws, and which is most relevantly found in Hoggart's freely acknowledged sources in Matthew Arnold and D.H. Lawrence. In this tradition (which has a substantial American counterpart in the work of literary intellectuals like Lionel Trilling or the 'New Critics', and the historian Daniel Boorstin) modern, industrial history is understood as tragedy, and twentieth-century consumer culture is the latest and most pernicious form of the resulting anarchy of values. In *The Uses of Literacy*, therefore, the plight of the relatively affluent postwar working class is described in a language which has in fact (*contra* Passeron) very little to do with familiar use, but a great deal to do with pulpit denunciation and mass–cultural jeremiad. Commercial culture is a 'spiritual dry-rot', a 'shiny barbarism', 'invitations to self-indulgence', 'techniques of mutual indulgence', 'a vast Vanity Fair of shouting indulgences', 'a paralysis of the moral will which is settling upon many people', in which 'Anything goes and there is no scale', etcetera.[23]

The narrative pattern and conceptual structure of the book is one of cultural loss and 'robbery' (Hoggart, 17, 24, 243, 323), an apocalypse of complete 'aesthetic breakdown' and 'moral levelling' (Hoggart, 184, 247, 340). So, if *The Uses of Literacy* is dense with an attractively rich texture of lived experience, at another level this is mediated by tendentious conceptual and evaluative categories which, because they are unargued, are, in Barthes's terms, food for myth, not thought. That is to say, *The Uses of Literacy* displays a naivety – or a telling duplicity – in its methodologically unspecific attitude to language. In many ways *Mythologies* and *The Uses of Literacy* are similar in diagnosis. They share a pessimistic sense of the present, and of the collapse of individual agency; of the loss of cultural memory, and the establishment of an eternal present (as in *The Fashion System*: compare Hoggart, 189); both denounce the accelerating commodification and reification of values, and a world increasingly constructed in the mythic image of 'the American way of life'; and both also – though more in Hoggart than in Barthes – are nostalgic for a time when language and experience were more gratifyingly integral.[24] But despite these similarities, the mood and attitude of the two books are very different. Barthes has none of the moral earnestness of Hoggart; *Mythologies* finds pleasure as well as cant in the consumer world, and this endeared him to younger British commentators.

The Uses of Literacy, by contrast, is a book embedded in a native tradition, and its language, for all its telling familiarity, is complicit with an analysis which cannot do other than condemn its materials (and its populations) to outer darkness. As has often been noted, Hoggart's book seems to break in half: the first part (as Passeron says) combats the ignorant ethnocentrism of many commentators on working-class experience, but the second draws the analysis, as it were, back into the nineteenth-century habit of judgemental spectatorship on working-class life. As Hoggart the adult academic squirms in new milk-bars, among 'the nastiness of their modernistic knick-knacks, their glaring showiness' (Hoggart, 247), he appears, for all his reasoned good sense, unable to get a relevant purchase on modernity. It is in this context that the advantages of Barthes's language and method are evident, and explain why his work on popular culture has been much more influential than the seemingly more secure tradition in which Hoggart worked. In the 1950s in Britain Hoggart's style of argument was everywhere – in Leavisite criticism, in the plays of Arnold Wesker or the novels of David Storey, and in the thinking of many educationalists, social workers and churchmen like Chad Varah (the founder of the Samaritans), who established the *Eagle* to combat the moral horrors of the American comics imported for servicemen. But for the most part, as with the Leavises, this mode of analysis retreated into a stony-faced opposition, which is one reason why contemporary debates about popular culture so often refuse to start from a point other than its threat to 'Culture'.

In *No Respect*, Andrew Ross's excellent study of modern attitudes to popular culture, he notes the persistence of the same model among both left- and right-wing opponents of capitalism. Both positions remain 'unswervingly loyal to their respective narratives of decline'.[25] Within these debates, however, Barthes is oddly situated and, not for the first time, does not conform to the usual patterns. His pessimism, for instance, is not essentially of the 'decline' variety. He insists that *all* structures are inevitably coercive, and that the past cannot be separated from the present, nor 'high' culture from 'low', in such a way that the two first terms are exempt from ideology's distortions. Barthes is, of course, highly judgemental, but his analytic method does not depend (as in Leavis or Hoggart) upon moral judgement. More important still, perhaps, is the skittish freedom he allows himself in his fascinated, detailed responses to consumer products or popular ritual. That is, Barthes seems in *Mythologies* (but not in *The Fashion System*) to *play* with the consumer toyshop of modern culture. Though in 'Toys' he complains that modern toys are too instrumental, too mimetic of 'real life', unlike their old-fashioned wooden counterparts (*Myth*, 53–5), none the less he has great fun playing creatively with their graceless equivalents in the modern world. Modern toys, he argues, imitate a world already formed; they cannot encourage 'poetic' discovery. But it seems to me, that it is just this kind of sportive, imaginative activity which Barthes is undertaking among the detergents, film actors and newspapers of contemporary France. If *Mythologies*, like much early Barthes, confronts us with a formal pessimism, it also gives us an informal demonstration of the very creative malleability of 'reality' which, he states, seems to be evaporating from the rigidities of the mythological world.

It is here that Barthes joins a rival, largely non-literary tradition of response to popular culture in this period which was particularly associated with the visual and plastic arts. I am thinking specifically of the London 'Independent Group' and, more widely, of the slightly later phenomenon of 'Pop' art across the West, which also made playful use of the junk and ephemera of mass communications. The 'Independent Group', or IG (a group of artists and architects, including Richard Hamilton and Eduardo Paolozzi, associated with the Institute of Contemporary Arts in the early 1950s), flaunted their contempt for 'high' culture by revelling in Hollywood, science fiction, advertising, automobiles and fashion to destabilise established definitions of 'art' and 'culture'. Like Barthes, IG refused moral commentary in their utilisation of American comic books or pulp fiction, and they plundered this 'image trove' as a way of dismantling the austere rigidities of academic art. Like several groups throughout Europe, IG were in search of a consciously modern internationalism which would subvert postwar establishments, and they drew substantially on European surrealism, Futurism and Dada as well as the 'new frontier' of American popular products.[26] Though they were much less explicitly political than Barthes, members of IG saw themselves as engaged in the same kind of iconoclastic playfulness with images which made use of irony and comic exuberance to deflate official 'Culture' in a way which became widespread in the 1960s in avant-garde or 'underground' circles.

It was this sense of being in tune with the contemporary which appealed to early enthusiasts for Barthes's work in Britain. John Berger, another author who moved easily between the visual and written arts, enthusiastically reviewed the English translation of *Mythologies* in 1972, praising the unprecedented clarity of its engagement with the present.[27] In the same year, his enormously influential *Ways of Seeing* set out a sequence of Barthesian points about institutionalised perception and art. The innovations of *Ways of Seeing* (the television tie-in, the juxtaposition of 'high' art with pornography and advertising, the abandonment of directive argument for the stark fragment or visual 'essay', the insistence that 'all images are man-made' and should be forced to reveal their acculturation) seem to follow closely Barthes's work in *Mythologies*. And it is crucial to see this network of ideas extending and inspiring work not just in criticism, but in creative writing too. In the next chapter we will look at Barthes's involvement with the avant-garde literary journal *Tel Quel*, but it is worth pointing out that there were also relevant developments in Britain. Berger's own experiments with alternative narrative modes in his novels and screenplays – the use of photographs, for instance, or a mode of composition in fragmentary episodes, as in his film *In the Middle of the World* – are, again, close to the thinking about form which Barthes developed in his poststructuralist work. The effort to break up old ways of seeing became a cultural habit.

In his review of the English *Mythologies*, Berger compared it with some recent essays in *New Society* by the novelist Angela

Carter which were subsequently collected in Carter's *Nothing Sacred* (1982) and a *New Society* collection – *Arts in Society* (1977) – compiled by the magazine's editor, Paul Barker, in which, once again, the connection was made with *Mythologies*. Carter's essays – on Japan, British popular ritual, style, fashion, erotica, and so on – are, if less thorough in analytic method, strikingly similar in mode of observation to Barthes's work. But more important, perhaps, is the strong relationship between the demythologising project Barthes set up in *Mythologies* and Carter's fiction. In 'Notes from the front line', an essay from 1983, Carter writes that artists do not have the legislative influence which Shelley is (wrongly) thought to have attributed to them. Instead, they investigate 'the social fictions which regulate our lives'. Artists question the 'versions of reality' which they inherit, and writing is a kind of 'applied linguistics' in the service of the 'demythologising business', a 'decolonialising of our language'.[28]

It is not difficult to see how close this project is, not just to Barthes, but to a whole movement in writing in the latter part of the twentieth century: as Carter acknowledges, what she is doing is similar to the work of 'Third World' writers reworking their imperial legacy. In Carter and these writers we see a sophisticated, knowing version of a literary principle adopted by Barthes and known as 'intertextuality'. We shall come to this in more detail in the next chapter, but it is important to see it – and the related process of demythologising – as one which joins creative and critical thinking. (Indeed, in much modern work it is unclear where the one begins and the other ends.) In 'Notes from the front line' Carter stresses how, in the absence of any authentic 'peasant' mythology, she uses Western literature as a mythological backcloth in relation to which her fictions develop their meanings. That is to say, her work is intertextually related to its traditions in a teasing but serious play. How Barthes developed his thinking in relation to this new playful sophistication will be the subject of Chapter 3.

CHAPTER
THREE

Works and texts:
poststructural Barthes

Hot roses: Barthes's poststructuralism

Most commentators on Barthes agree that his work took a significantly different turn towards the end of the 1960s, and that this is indicative – indeed, partially creative – of the division between structuralism and what has become known as poststructuralism. Poststructuralism developed in part from a critique of structuralism, but continued to insist that the analysis of language is central to any modern intellectual project. Poststructuralist developments by, among others, Foucault, Lacan, Barthes and the new Parisian 'master' Jacques Derrida, founder of 'deconstruction', took different directions, but all questioned the model of language which Barthes used in 'Myth today' and *The Fashion System*. In poststructuralism, language is no longer seen as a reliable yardstick for the measurement of other signifying systems. It is now seen as itself an impossible medium. This development follows a pattern within modern theories of knowledge, which often move from an 'objectivist' stance to one which challenges the assumptions underlying 'objectivity' itself. For structuralists, the language model is an obedient animal which pulls the analytic caravan quietly. For poststructuralist thinkers, language is much too frisky for this.

Any major shift in intellectual opinion has multiple causes, and the overall social and cultural changes between the 1950s and the late-1960s clearly played a major role in the transition to poststructuralism, as will be made clear later. But this section will concentrate on the evolution of Barthes's structuralism from within the analysis of literature itself. For if his previous work had attacked literature as a privileged category, his poststructuralism recovers it as a special, but representative, condition of language. The reason for this is easy to see if we take the example of the mythology of roses used in Chapter 2 a little further. In 'Myth today' Barthes argued that mythological roses signifying passion suppress certain of the connotative possibilities of roses (thorns, greenfly, canker) and promote others (sweet smell, beauty, blooming health). Thus a positive signifying mythology for love is created based on a kind of repression. But many uses of mythological roses are not so straightforward. Uses can be ironic, for instance, or explore complex associations – as, for instance, in George Herbert's poem 'Vertue', which makes use of the plant's mortality and other associations of redness like anger. Similarly, Angela Carter's rewritings of fairy stories in *The Bloody Chamber* (1979) use countermythological associations to build complex patterns of desire, loss, cruelty, and so forth.

Structuralist analysis can therefore bring a helpful analytic clarity to relatively simple systems, but threatens to become helplessly reductive before more complicated phenomena. Blake's poem 'The Sick Rose' from *Songs of Innocence and of Experience* (1794) provides an example:

O Rose thou art sick.
The invisible worm,
That flies in the night
In the howling storm:

Has found out thy bed
Of crimson joy:
And his dark secret love
Does thy life destroy.

This poem clearly makes use of the convention that roses signify passion – indeed, it is impossible to follow the poem at all without a knowledge of it. But, equally clearly, it also unsettles this convention and breaks down the simple emblematic mode by deploying many more layers of signification than the first-order, second-order model of *Mythologies* allows. The significatory resources of this poem are, as ever in Blake, vastly out of proportion to its brevity, bearing in mind that Blake conceived it as a visual as well as a verbal experience, and printed it in a pictorial design which has a palpable but not immediately clear relationship to the text. In addition, the poem is in dialectical relationship with companion poems in the 'Songs of Innocence' which mirror and question the 'Experience' poems in the composite volume *Songs of Innocence and of Experience*. So the whole ensemble of significations is quarrelsomely related to the mythic simplicity of roses. But this is not a mere contradiction of the mythology. What is 'said' about love is a matter of debate, but it is not a simple refutation: 'You think love is sweet, but it isn't'. The poem provokes questions and problems; it does not participate in neat alignments of meaning. Why is the worm invisible? Why is his sickly relationship with the rose described as one of love? and so on. This kind of complex ambiguity will not settle into the straightforward patterns in which the structuralist vulgate of popular cultural analysis specialised.

The critique of literary structuralism from this kind of position began early in France. Paul de Man, later one of the doyens of American deconstruction, criticised Barthes's strictly prestructuralist *Writing Degree Zero* in these terms as early as 1954. Perceptively spotting that Barthes's work was becoming increasingly formalist, de Man took him to task for underestimating the plurality and complexity of literary language. Barthes's emphasis on the confiscation of literature by 'Literature' underestimates its resistance to tight codes, and for de Man (as for many poststructuralists subsequently, including Barthes himself) it is literature's perverse polysemy which is crucial to it.[1] De Man returned to this theme in 1972 in an essay that was not published until after his death. In it he continued to argue that Barthes's oversimplified structuralism actually prevented him from seeing that, in literary works, language functions in a way that cannot be accounted for by 'scientific semiology'.[2]

De Man puts one version of the radical poststructuralist case. For him, Barthes's innovations in the study of literary language were (at least by 1972) 'relatively slight', and his structuralism ignored the 'autotelic, nonreferential aspect of literature'.

However, for others, like Julia Kristeva – who had once been Barthes's student – his work had more valuable resources. Reviewing his work in 1971, she too was critical of structuralism: 'the technicist illusion that "literary science" need only reproduce the norms of science (if possible, linguistics . . .) . . . in order to insert itself into the dignified but amorphous domain of "studies in mass communications"'.[3] But it is clear that Kristeva was trying to construct a new view of Barthes to speak to a new line of enquiry. This Barthes is a 'laboratory of a new discourse', an experiment in modern styles and methods. Structuralism was a plaything which, soon exhausted, produced (in a common, and somewhat gruesome, metaphor used sometimes by Barthes himself) a 'mutation', a wholly new biological strand which would triumph evolutionarily but at present appeared strange and unwelcome.

Kristeva's essay was written for *Tel Quel* ('As it is'), a militant, avant-garde journal centred on Kristeva's husband, the novelist and theorist Philippe Sollers. *Tel Quel* was an often bizarre but none the less influential mixture of literary and theoretical experimentalism and political radicalism which, in a very '1960s' manner, purposefully blurred these distinctions. Barthes, and other poststructuralist luminaries associated with the journal, like Derrida, developed theoretical positions to attack the intellectual establishment.[4] Kristeva's Barthes is therefore a radical Barthes who, as 'capitalist society is economically and politically choked to death' (Kristeva, 92), coupled ideological critique of the 'literary machine' to the 'resistance' of avant-garde language. For Kristeva, Barthes did appreciate those elements of literary language de Man thought he neglected; but she set them in the social context of an embattled avant-garde which alone keeps the power of literary language alive in the significatory graveyard of decadent capitalism.

For Kristeva, literature is pliant and generous. It retains its integrity while playing host to 'all the hypotheses of the human sciences; it gives the linguist as well as the historian its surplus value, on condition that it remains in the shadows of knowledge as a passive thing, never an agent' (Kristeva, 95). Adapting Barthes's argument in *Writing Degree Zero*, she distinguishes more sharply still between literature and criticism. For her, literature is an innocent substance co-opted and distorted by the masterful discourses of linguistics, history and criticism. It thus provides an image of political possibility; a resistant, destabilising, ever-generative presence: 'From within "structuralism", Barthes was probably the first to consider language as negativity, less because of a philosophical option (deconstruction, antimetaphysics, etc.) than by reason of the very object of his investigation' (Kristeva, 107). In short, it was because his 'object of investigation' was literature itself that Barthes came to his critique of ideology, not the other way round.

For Kristeva, Barthes turns structuralism inside out. If structuralism was based on the model of *langue*, poststructuralism is based on avant-garde *parole*, whose 'negativity' corrodes authority. The role of literature is therefore liberatory: 'For subjects of a civilisation who are alienated in their language and blocked by their history, the work of Barthes shows that literature is precisely the place where this alienation and this blockage are thwarted each time in a specific way' (Kristeva, 96). Literature, therefore, is recalled to a familiar salvationary role in culture, but not as an alternative value structure asserted against the dominant as was the case with Leavis, or indeed with Barthes's notional Marxism in some of his earlier work. In its uniqueness and negative capability, literature is a microcosm of the desirable human good because its relaxed negativity images a better world and dissolves the assertive claims of masterful discourses.

This political argument forms the backdrop to the institutional presence of Barthes's poststructuralism, but Kristeva's account is important for other reasons. As Barthes fulsomely acknowledged, it was Kristeva who refreshed his sense of the signifying potential of literature, and made available the more generative idea of language which lay behind it.[5] In her essay on Barthes, Kristeva wrote: 'Any sentence is both syntax and nonsentence, normative unicity and disorderly multiplicity; any sequence is both myth and the melting pot where it is engendered and dies through its own history . . . ' (Kristeva, 99). This is a little obscure in the details, but the overall sense is clear. Language both creates structure and meaning, and radically destabilises it; it creates and uses myth, but also dismantles it; and it is easy to see the relevance of this to the Blake poem we examined above. But what is also interesting is Kristeva's choice of metaphors of heat (the melting pot) and biological fecundity, because their connotations are strikingly similar to those used by Barthes himself in *Writing Degree Zero* to describe literary 'style'. It is as if, in this period, Barthes shifts his attention from chilly institutionalised 'Literature' to the fugitive but positive element he called 'style' in the earlier work. However, this later feature (relabelled 'Text' or simply 'writing', and later still reconnected with the body, as we shall see in Chapter 4) is dispossessed of the new frontier. In the world now pictured by Barthes and Kristeva alike, there are no fresh territories. It is a world covered over entirely by orthodoxy:

> Everything suggests that we cannot escape: by culture, by political choice, we must be committed, engage in one of the particular languages to which our world, our history compels us. And yet we cannot renounce the gratification – however utopian – of a de-situated, dis-alienated language. Thus we must hold in the same hand the two reins of commitment and gratification, must assume a plural philosophy of languages. ('The war of languages', 1973; *Rustle*, 109)

The old Sartrean problematic of commitment remains entirely on the plane of language itself, and, as for many 1960s radicals, engagement and gratification become one and the same by slipping past the determinations of history. In the idea of avant-garde literary language proposed by Kristeva, and enthusiastically adopted by Barthes, the utopia of plurality, and the critique by 'negativity', are happily combined.

It is tempting to see a connection between this development and Barthes's altered status within intellectual Paris. After the Picard affair had died away, and with a growing reputation, Barthes was now both dissident and insider in French academic life. In the same way, avant-garde writing is both within the cultural mainstream of intellectual Paris, and obliquely and critically situated towards it. This is one reason why both Barthes and Kristeva are fond of images of borders, margins, edges, and a permanent mobility in tight spaces. It is as if this new writing is a metaphoric rendering of a few streets in certain *arrondissements*. On the broader map of Barthes's development, there is no longer an alternative *to* 'Literature' in some distant frontier of the imagination. Instead there is an alternative *within* it to be found on the unstable fault lines between the individual and history, 'nature' and 'culture', chance and necessity, subjective and objective (all these are taken from Kristeva's essay). In the new poststructural theory, it is these edges which the play of signification exploits.

The change in Barthes's critical methodology after the collapse of structuralism is easy to illustrate. In 1971 he wrote retrospectively of *Mythologies* in 'Mythology today'. Though he doubted that the nature of myth had changed, ways of understanding it had. Myth, therefore, was 'a different object', and structuralist demystification had itself become a perverse kind of myth of rationalistic analysis. The need now, therefore, was to think about density of signification, not decipherment. But he preserved an old project too: the analysis of what, following Lacan, he called 'the Imaginary', the network of mythic representations with and through which most lives are led. But it is now the psychological density of their impact which interests him, not their ideological demerit (*IMT*, 165–70). As we shall see in Chapter 4, this new interest in the psychological accommodations with myth represents as powerful a shift in focus for Barthes as does the shift from a structural to a poststructural view of language.

The change is also clear in his analysis of narrative. Having set out a structural model in 1966 in relation to *Goldfinger*, his subsequent analyses explore its limits and possibilities. In line with the new conception of language he was exploring in this period, Barthes finds that the structural model is unable to sustain the search for a universal 'grammar' of narrative announced in 'Introduction to the structuralist analysis of narrative'. The prime example of this is his best-known book of literary analysis, *S/Z*, to which we shall come shortly. But a succinct indication of structuralism's difficulties is the essay 'The struggle with the angel: textual analysis of Genesis 32:22–32' (1971). This takes a brief piece of biblical narrative – the story of Jacob wrestling with the angel – and demonstrates just why it is not susceptible to structural analysis. Like Blake's 'The Sick Rose', it baffles an analysis which tries to reduce it to structural proportion because it has a 'sequential readability but cultural ambiguity' (it casts an odd light on God's role in the world, for instance). Barthes is no longer interested in structural description but in the 'savour' (a carefully chosen non-scientific, almost dilettante word) of the story's ambiguities and hesitations:

> what interests me in this famous passage is not the 'folkloristic' model but the abrasive frictions, the breaks, the discontinuities of readability, the juxtaposition of narrative entities which have to some extent run free from an explicit logical articulation. (*IMT*, 140)

As this passage makes clear, Barthes's language will now rely more on metaphors of dysfunction than of structural efficiency. He is interested in the points where the model breaks down, and language seizes hold of a structural or aesthetic pattern. For him these ten verses are an 'open-network', a 'very infinity of language'; the story is 'structured without closure', 'it explodes, disseminates' (*IMT*, 126–7). No doubt there is a deliberate impishness in Barthes's choice of the Bible to expose the way language undermines truth and authority.

Another essay of the period, on Jules Verne's *Mysterious Island*, has the symptomatic title 'Where to begin?' (1970). This essay is interesting because it crosses rhetorics from two overlapping phases. Structuralism, Barthes writes, has no 'canonical method'; its task is 'to accomplish . . . the text's *plural*' (*NCE*, 79). What is striking is that this 'structuralist' method sounds entirely like its successor. That is, 'Where to begin?', like *S/Z* from the same year, is written at a cusp in Barthes's career when the terminology of structuralism is still naming a method which is in fact undermining its credentials. This terminological confusion was one reason for the perplexity about what structuralism was which persisted in Britain long after it had been abandoned by many of its French partisans. Just at the moment when British minds were being turned towards it, it was vanishing into the heady play of poststructuralist language. But *S/Z* – widely thought in Britain to be 'structuralist' – is itself not exactly clear about where the one undertaking begins and the other ends, and its opening pages are a complex compendium of projects old and new.

S/Z is a dramatic and ingenious reworking of a novella by Balzac, *Sarrasine*, which tells the story of the young, eponymous artist who falls in love with a singer, La Zambinella. What is different about this conventional theme is that La Zambinella is eventually revealed to be a man, a castrato, and the narrative ends with Sarrasine's death in shame and horror at the hands of a rival. This story is framed, however, by one in which the narrator tries to barter the tale for an evening's passion with a young woman. This affair is also doomed because of the woman's disgust at the spectacle of castration. So the tale groups a number of Barthesian themes: the way reality is hidden beneath screens of delusion, the way art masks reality in the cases of both La Zambinella himself, and Sarrasine's 'realistic' sculpture of his loved one which proves true only to appearances. Finally, the bargain between the narrator and the young woman appears to Barthes to represent the mercantile exchange, and inevitable disappointment, which lies at the root of all traditional narrative.

What Barthes does with Balzac's story cannot really be considered orthodox criticism, though it has all the *appearance* of a full commentary on *Sarrasine* in the manner of traditional 'practical criticism' or 'explication de texte'. Barthes divides the thirty-odd-page novella into 561 pieces (or 'lexia') and provides what seems to be a specific commentary on each. These are assembled into 93 numbered units with puckish, enigmatic titles: 'Connotation: for, even so'; 'The castrato's posterity'; 'Very natural actions' and the Magritte-ish 'This is not an "explication de texte"', for instance. The analysis is conducted through the indentification of five 'codes' which, Barthes claims, organise the experience of reading. These are the HERMENEUTIC code (the code which provokes questions of interpretation); the code of the SEME (referring to the network of connotation of metaphors, allusions, and so forth); the code of the SYMBOLIC (the structures of symbolic oppositions – light and dark, for instance); the code of ACTION (the 'logic' of events); and the code of REFERENCE (the system of references to cultural codes and commonplace knowledge about places, events, social circles, stereotyped psychology, and so on). At first sight these seem to have an impressively solid, structuralist aura: Barthes gives them abbreviations – HER, SEM, SYM, ACT, REF – and works through a system of stars, numbers and diagrams which gives the appearance, at least, of scientific rigour (though they also remind one of a bizarrely obsessive mystical commentary). The whole is quite purposefully offered as a sort of musical score for a serial composition in which numerical and other sequences take the place of the developed structural properties of traditional melodic and harmonic forms. (Barthes was himself an accomplished pianist and understood, and was much interested in, music.)

But the structuralist apparatus, and its occasional use of 'structuralist' notions (for instance, that 'character' is created by the mere repetition of semes – see *S/Z*, 67), is contradicted by a method which flaunts its arbitrariness. The SEMIC code, for instance, is not, Barthes writes, very thorough. It is 'unstable'. Semes are followed like 'motes of dust, flickers of meaning' (*S/Z*, 19). Similarly Barthes writes of the lexias themselves as 'arbitrary in the extreme' (*S/Z*, 13), and of the operation as one of '*man-handling* the text, *interrupting* it' to deny its cohesion (*S/Z*, 15). The whole effect he compares to that of 'a minor earthquake' (*S/Z*, 13). So there are very contradictory signals in *S/Z*. Whereas structuralist analysis tried to follow the functional workings of a text (and by implication, therefore, respected its integrity), what is happening in *S/Z* is an ultra-radicalisation of *Sarrasine*, a sort of cultural re-education somewhat in the Chinese manner. (Like many Parisian intellectuals in this period, Barthes briefly flirted with Maoism.)

Barthes begins by attacking the structuralist analysis of narrative he had done so much to promote, because it assumes that all narratives are fundamentally the same, and can be resolved into their structural foundations. This means a loss of *difference*, by which he means not the unique 'irreducible quality' of literary creation (which he thinks is a myth) but the 'infinity' of language itself, which produces more meaning than can be counted in structuralist bookkeeping (*S/Z*, 3). Furthermore, narrative itself has a dubious role in modern culture. The common forms of narrative are now so insidiously ubiquitous that they unconsciously shape our perceptions. The common narratives become 'cultural models' which form our understanding of history, for instance, or the way the economy works (*S/Z*, 52). The response, therefore, must be not to accede to narrative (as structuralism quietly did) but to check it and reverse its usual 'force' (a frequent metaphor in *S/Z*). Readers of narrative – and *Sarrasine* is offered as a 'classic', typical narrative – need to stop being passive consumers, and become active creators of their own 'Texts'. *S/Z* is in one sense a rallying cry to the restive couch potatoes of the Western narrative tradition.

S/Z, therefore, is a book about empowerment, and this was the dominant way it was read in Britain in the 1970s (Rosalind Coward and John Ellis's *The Language of Materialism* [1977] is an austere example). This was one reason for the hostility with which a misunderstood 'structuralism' was regarded in some quarters, but there are other dimensions to it. One is that *S/Z* is actually addressing a very common and very direct experience of reading. In an essay written in the same year, 'Writing reading' (1970), Barthes notes that narrative is actually not read at the level of action alone. One stops and thinks, so that the 'onward' experience is continually checked by the 'flow of ideas, stimuli, associations'. 'In a word,' Barthes asks, 'haven't you ever happened *to read while looking up from your book?*' (*Rustle*, 29). He goes on to say that *S/Z* reads *Sarrasine* as if it were 'filmed in slow motion'. The composition is there, but what interests him is the stimulation of thought which occurs in the pause between one sequence and the next. Composition '*channels*', he remarks, whereas reading '*disperses*' in a kind of 'game' with the text. So the fragmentary dismantling of the narrative of *Sarrasine*, and its '*step-by-step*' remaking in the mind of the reader (*S/Z*, 12), is in a sense a re-creation of the process of reading itself. Though this takes liberties with the text's integrity, it is also a responsible acknowledgement of the mental processes involved in reading, and this experiential dimension to *S/Z*, often overlooked, is surely one of the book's principal appeals.

One reason, perhaps, why it is so little noticed is that Barthes glosses it with a deliberately provoking polemic, and *S/Z* adds an infusion of earlier existential agitations to his cocktail of structuralist and poststructuralist rhetorics. Reading is irredeemably solitary and morally uncomfortable. It demands an existential choice to be either producer or consumer, active or passive, authentic or inauthentic, free or not, plurally creative or (with a glance at *Mythologies* and *The Fashion System*) a victim 'plasticised by a singular system' (*S/Z*, 4–5). This existential strand runs throughout *S/Z*, and Barthes characterises 'classic' narrative in a familiar way. He attacks the way ' "life", in the classic text, becomes a nauseating mixture of common opinions, a smothering layer of received ideas' (*S/Z*, 206); he protests at the 'bad faith' and casuistry of classic writing, which proposes false enigmas only to solve them within conventional understanding (*S/Z*, 141); and finally he objects to the construction of a pseudo-freedom for characters who are actually always at the mercy of narrative conventions and conventional psychology (*S/Z*, 135).

This last theme was, once again, common in the period. It is anticipated in the formal structuring of John Fowles's *The French Lieutenant's Woman* (1969), for instance, which makes reference to Barthes's work to justify its departures from 'classic' form (see the beginning of Chapter 13). However, Fowles's work – for all its stress on choice, existential freedom and game-playing – would certainly not have been the kind of avant-garde 'Text' Barthes had in mind. To put it simply, *The French Lieutenant's Woman*'s language is too enslaved by the conventions of nineteenth-century fiction which it seeks to imitate and parody. In *S/Z*, Barthes comments that parody and irony are in fact insufficiently transgressive and multivalent (*S/Z*, 44–5).

So *S/Z* resumes concerns addressed in *Writing Degree Zero* (the 'classic' is 'Literature') and *Mythologies* (the 'classic' is myth), but in a much more eclectic, hybrid way. Its calculated outrageousness of generalisation and language, its polyglot of theoretical diction and whimsical metaphor, are part of the book's brio and attack. The critical activity is described not as interpretation (still less as explication) but as an 'appreciation' of the plurality of writing (*S/Z*, 5). The term has a calculatedly old-fashioned ring to it, and in 'Theory of the text' (1973) Barthes welcomes the return of the amateur to combat the stultification of institutional criticism ('Theory', 42). So here is a further lively contradiction: *S/Z* manipulates the technocriticism of modern structuralism and poststructuralism, but also harks back to a belletrist world of the occasional essay and the enthusiasms of the man of letters. In a political sense this contradiction is disabling (it is difficult to reconcile the Marxist and the gentleman of taste), but it is representative of a complex 'postmodern' cultural habit found also in the 'heritage' industry, 'electronic cottages', and the like.

This assembly of styles is reflected in the imagery, and *S/Z* has a virtuosity of language which enacts its theme that reading is actually a form of creative writing. The argument, indeed, sometimes seems to be conducted almost entirely by a flow of rival images characterising, on the one hand, the playful adventure of poststructural language, and, on the other, the sealed-up world of the 'classic' system. The latter is described with the heavy inflections of the radicalism of the period. It is the discourse of authority; it is like God; it is like the operation of the legal system or the circulation of goods in capitalist economies. 'Classic' discourse, in Barthes's rhetoric, is a mean discourse of unwavering parsimony in which the flow of significatory merchandise is regulated by the iron 'force' of the codes: 'it is a force which attempts to subjugate other forces, other meanings, other languages' (*S/Z*, 154).

'Textual' or 'writerly' discourse (the opposite of 'classic' or 'readerly' discourse) is evoked in a flurry of calculatedly inconsistent metaphors, as if the nature of poststructuralist language can only be unstable. Many of these deliberately overturn the images used for the 'classic'. If the 'classic' has its commodities, the 'Textual' is like things which cannot be possessed, or even desired, like holes, gaps and fragments, or things which halt the circulation of meaning (*S/Z*, 74). If the 'classic' is metaphorically described as a world of solid, stable objects (buildings, places, reliable 'characters'), the 'Textual' is the world of the open air, the migrations of animals, the flights of birds, the random outcroppings of rock, passages across difficult terrain, the leaping of walls. It is a wandering world, not the 'organised drift' of 'classic' reading: the domain of collapse, not solid structure. Hence the language of earthquake, conflagration, scattering, explosion, unravelling, breaking, the shard and the fragment.

'Classic' writing is built in 'blocks' cemented together with 'logical paste' (*S/Z*, 156); its meanings are gathered in comely order 'around the hearth of denotation (the hearth: center, guardian, refuge, light of truth)' (*S/Z*, 7). But if 'classic' writing is metaphorically the bourgeois home, the 'Text' is a surreal space – a maze, a room without doors, a network with a thousand entrances (*S/Z*, 65, 12). The space of the 'Text' expands and contracts; it is the dust in a room or the very galaxy itself (S/Z, 5). Many of Barthes's images are visual; it is as if the 'Text' shrinks and expands, appears and disappears in vanishing points, cinematic decompositions, slow motions, dissolves, mirages and receding perspectives. The 'Text', indeed, is plural, playful and infinite. It has no boundaries and cannot, Barthes says, be bought as a book. It is an intertextual freewheel. In a striking image, it is composed not of blocks but of 'polyhedrons faceted by a word' (*S/Z*, 14). That is, its significations, in the slow turning of 'Textual' reading, produce an infinity of facets for examination.

S/Z dazzles – partly because it is designed to enact the radical initiatives its argument proposes, and partly because it seeks to reconceive the mental landscape in which modern writing should be read. Recently, George Landow has argued that 'In *S/Z*, Roland Barthes describes an ideal textuality that precisely matches that which has come to be called computer hypertext – text composed of blocks of words (or images) linked electronically by multiple paths, chains, or trails in an open-ended, perpetually unfinished textuality described by the terms *link, node, network, web*, and *path*', and his suggestion is very fruitful.[6] What *S/Z* proposes is not a critical method as such, but a new environment for criticism which is distinctively and constitutively modern. This, perhaps, is why there are relatively few analytic 'tools' one can take from *S/Z*, despite its close-focus commitment to the micro-level of Balzac's tale. What *S/Z* seeks to establish is not a method in the structuralist sense but an attitude or approach. It defines a condition – of contemporary writing and reading – and sets in motion an imagistic vocabulary for its description. It remains, therefore, in the next section, to explore the capacities and limits of this new environment.

The arts of pleasure and noise

The issues raised in *S/Z* preoccupied Barthes for the remainder of his career. They might be divided into two areas: those which concern the definition of the literary object, the 'Text', and those which bear upon the subjectivity of the reader. The first of these will concern us for the remainder of this chapter before we turn, in Chapter 4, to the redefinition of subjectivity. But it is important to understand from the start that the two are directly related, and that Barthes and others envisaged a radical redefinition of the terms by which we understand the connection between them. For Barthes, the argument turns upon the newly envisioned possibilities offered by literature itself.

'Text' is, in many ways, a difficult notion to grasp. Indeed, it seems to have been a principle that 'Text' is only evocable, and cannot be described. It is not a formal object in the way, say, that a sonnet is or a tragedy. In 'Theory of the text' Barthes writes that 'Text' transgresses generic boundaries, and that it 'can be approached by definitions, but also (and perhaps above all) by metaphors' ('Theory', 35–6). In other words, 'Text' has an inherent generic instability, and invites a creative conjuration as much as critical definition. Indeed, 'Text' sometimes seems to be a kind of black hole for criticism, a point where conventional analytic language disappears into a different, crushed dimension. What is at stake with 'Text', therefore, is as much an experience and attitude as any formal analysis. This makes it unstable and controversial as a critical concept in a profession which puts a high, but anxious, price on objectivity. In turn this instability is mirrored in a confusion in Barthes's own definitions. He hesitates between implying that 'Texts' are literary objects different in kind from other less rich and exciting works, and definitions which imply that 'Text' is to be found wherever one seeks it because its foundation is psychological. Sometimes Barthes writes in this manner: 'all one can say is that in such-and-such a work, there is, or there isn't, some Text' ('Theory', 39), which seems to imply that 'Text' can be spotted, like trains or butterflies. But one contradictory lesson of *S/Z* is that 'Text' is discovered by excavating the extreme signifying density of *all* literary language. After all, as is often noted, *S/Z* purports to examine a 'classic' work, but mines it so thoroughly that the 'classic' ends up looking like a piece of 'Text'.

Nevertheless, 'Text' has several fairly consistent properties. The first is that it is strictly severed from intention, origin and even author. 'Text' is an action in language, not an act of intended meaning. The 'Text', therefore, signals (in one of Barthes's most successful polemical utterances) 'The death of the author', an idea he shared with Foucault as well as the *Tel Quel* group. The author, for these thinkers, is a commercial agent; what is important is the writer, because writers (by circular definition) challenge orthodoxy and celebrate plurality. 'Text' cannot belong to institutions as authors do (an echo of an old theme from *Writing Degree Zero*); therefore it cannot be destroyed. Its resources are a perpetual motion of signifying possibilities which suggest an ancient alchemy or a modern ecological utopia, as in the essay 'The death of the author' itself (1968). Here 'Text' comes from 'innumerable centres'; its signifying productivity has 'no halt'; it 'ceaselessly posits meaning, ceaselessly to evaporate it'; its very being is multiplicity (*IMT*, 146–7).

The activity of 'Textual' analysis, therefore, is a kind of play which is endlessly repeatable with different outcomes, partly depending on how much of the 'intertext' one decides to feed in. For 'Text' is not confinable to single books. It flows out and back, from 'Text' to 'Text', like (in a favourite metaphor in *S/Z*) the forces which hold stars together in constellation. At the other end of the scale, there is a captivation by details, frequently at the expense of larger patterns of argument, and a fascination with the materials and means of writing itself: letters and alphabets (as in *S/Z*), puns, strange words and neologisms, things which call attention to, as it were, the signifier and not the conventional signified. They force the reader to attend to the language and not automatically decode the meaning.[7]

Probably Barthes's fullest exploration of the idea of 'Text' comes in his essay-length book *The Pleasure of the Text* (1973). Like *S/Z*, *The Pleasure of the Text* is formally innovative, consisting of 46 brief *pensées* of as little as two lines which are loosely grouped thematically. Impishly, each *pensée* is named in the contents, but not in the text, so the whole has a circular meditatative feel which, rather like the arrangement of a subtle collection of poems, leaves the reader reaching for, without being confident of, the principles of organisation. The overall effect is, aptly, one of relaxed release, which is of course what Barthes intended. Following its drift, one need not worry so hard about coherence, ultimate meaning or the whole duty of interpretation which is so much a part of the professionalisation of literary criticism. In this respect *The Pleasure of the Text* is arrestingly different from the spiritual earnestness of much traditional Anglo-American criticism, which has often been suspicious of pleasure and sensuality. (F.R. Leavis's extraordinary essay on Keats in *Revaluation* is an example of this, though Leavis, Lawrence's champion, was inconsistent in this respect.) But once again, it has to be said that Barthes is contradictorily situated here. He himself was a zealous methodological innovator and, while proclaiming himself an amateur enthusiast, has been a handsome beneficiary of the new professionalism.

Following Kristeva, 'Text' is generous and accommodating. You cannot go 'wrong' with 'Text' – unless, that is, you try to wrench it from plurality into stereotype. As Barthes puts it, the 'Text' never denies, it only looks away (*PoT*, 3). Barthes asks us to imagine a man who has no sense of contradiction, in whom all languages cohabit without strain. This person is the reader of 'Text'. In 'Text', there is no longer any punishment for Babel, the confusion of tongues. There is only the celebratory relish of their differences (*PoT*, 4). However, if this dimension of 'Text' is euphorically utopian, another insists on the necessity of fall, for 'Text' is nothing if not oxymoronic. A person who lives in Babel must by definition, Barthes argues, live on the margins of a society which prizes a restrictive version of rationality. So if in one sense 'Text' is an image of generosity, it is also an enactment of loss. For what the reader experiences is not the reception of any old meaning, but the evaporation of the everyday certainty which caps 'Text' with imposed meaning. So the pleasure of the 'Text' is the jubilant pain of loss, and the reader experiencing it to the hilt must abandon social norms and conventional meanings. Once again, therefore, we hear a familiar Barthesian political rhythm. 'Text' is revolutionary because it is asocial; and it is asocial irrespective of the quality of the society in which it is experienced. 'Text' is necessarily the perverse, the excluded, the mad, the atopic, the hole which wrecks the exchange of cultural capital; 'it is the Text's very uselessness that is useful' (*PoT*, 24).

For Barthes, as for many 1960s radicals, pleasure is subversive of the *status quo*. But Barthes's ideas about pleasure are complex. For him pleasure is not gratification, because what is gratifying is usually a confirmation of existing identity. On the contrary, Barthes posits another state which he calls '*jouissance*', an untranslatable French word usually rendered as 'bliss', but perhaps having more of a sense of sexual ecstasy. *Jouissance*/bliss is a state of transport, an ecstatic loss of previous being. In *The Pleasure of the Text* Barthes carefully leaves the idea unfocused, as a psychological synonym for 'Text' itself: 'pleasure can be expressed in words, bliss cannot. Bliss is unspeakable, inter-dicted' (*PoT*, 21). Whereas pleasure loves the literal and the cultural, bliss is inevitably disruptive, kin to madness, a thrilling vertigo. So at the heart of the 'Textual' utopia is a radical instability which plays cat and mouse with the stable self. Though he looks for analogies in a somewhat modish view of madness, Barthes's significant point is that bliss is possible because the self returns to something like its original equilibrium. He posits a '"living contradiction"': a split subject, who simultaneously enjoys, through the Text, the consistency of his selfhood and its collapse, its fall' (*PoT*, 21). But the consequences of this for culture are stunning. Not only is the individual living a divided, unstable existence, but all culture is similarly fissured. '[I]f I believe', he writes,

> that pleasure and bliss are parallel forces, that they cannot meet, and that between them there is more than a struggle: an *incommunication*, then I must certainly believe that history, our history, is not peaceable and perhaps not even intelligent, that the Text of bliss always arises out of it like a scandal (an irregularity), that it is always the trace of a cut, of an assertion (and not of a flowering), and that the subject of this history (this historical subject that I am among others), far from being possibly pacified . . . is never anything but a 'living contradiction'. (*PoT*, 20–21)

This line of thinking originates in psychoanalysis, and throughout *The Pleasure of the Text* Barthes acknowledges his debt to Jacques Lacan. But this – at heart pessimistic – view of culture is traceable directly to Freud himself, and Barthes's sketch echoes the account of the function of culture in Freud's *Civilisation and its Discontents* (1929).

Freud's great book argues that human beings are inevitably disposed towards psychological and cultural dissatisfaction. The fact that the human constitution is weak, that humans have to battle against nature, and that their social relationships are inadequate, means that personality is created by the effort to reconcile instinctual drives and the demands of group living. Inevitably this means in turn that it is based on the suppression of conflict, and that repressed instinctual energies need to be reconciled with cultural norms. Failure to do so leads to neurosis. Cultural development, meanwhile, depends on recouping energy made available by repression. Culture is produced by 'draining off' this energy in the interests of the group. (The notorious theory that art is a sublimation of the sex drive is a vulgar form of this argument.) Culture therefore sets up a circuit in which its function is to mobilise reserves of energy created by repression to create further repression. At its gloomiest, Freud's scenario is one of inevitable illness.

This quick sketch cannot do justice to the full argument, but it is not difficult to see that Barthes, too, pictures culture as co-optive of human instincts. He too posits an antagonism between culture and the individual (revealed, for instance, in the images of conflict in the passage quoted above: cutting, contradiction, scandal, incommunication); and he too sees that moments of release are culturally disruptive. *The Pleasure of the Text*, then, founds its ecstatic celebrations on the basis of inevitable neurosis: 'every writer's motto reads: *mad I cannot be, sane I do not deign to be, neurotic I am*' (*PoT*, 6). Indeed, the maturity of the 'Text' of bliss is that it recognises frustration as inevitable but celebrates the desire which is the necessary adult condition because we cannot have all we demand. For Barthes, the immature text is that which 'prattles'; it is an 'unweaned language' which goes through 'the motions of ungratified sucking, of an undifferentiated orality' (*PoT*, 5). The prattling text (never defined by Barthes but, one supposes, a kind of equivalent to myth) tries to 'seduce' its reader.

The mature 'Text', on the other hand, plays a dangerous game on the edges. 'Neither culture nor its destruction is erotic,' Barthes writes; 'it is the seam between them, the fault, the flaw, which becomes so' (*PoT*, 7).

That the erotic is a moment of uncertainty is a major Barthesian theme. The erotic is not explicit but suspenseful. Hence the language of edges and margins in *S/Z* and *The Pleasure of the Text*: 'what pleasure wants is the site of a loss, the seam, the cut, the deflation, the *dissolve* which seizes the subject in the midst of bliss' (*PoT*, 7). Or, more bluntly: 'is not the most erotic portion of a body *where the garment gapes?*' (*PoT*, 9). Bliss is not the voyeuristic gratifications of the striptease. This is conventional pleasure (*PoT*, 10). It is the uncertain, unbalanced dialectic between fulfilment and loss, the possible and the interdicted, the safe and the vertiginous, which constitutes the real joy of writing as, for Barthes, of life.[8]

One of the difficulties of *The Pleasure of the Text* is that it confuses the usual operation of metaphor. In conventional metaphors, a subject is described (usually called the tenor) by reference to something different (usually called the vehicle). The common ground between them reveals something about the subject. In our regular example, when Burns writes 'My luve is like a red, red rose' the freshness of the rose is telling us something about the poet's love. But in *The Pleasure of the Text* it is never quite clear whether Barthes is talking about life or about writing, because the figurative pattern is disconcertingly reversible. Is the subject of the book literary writing and the vehicle sexual psychology, or the other way round? In this respect *The Pleasure of the Text* becomes a bit like those jackets which can be turned inside out so that the lining becomes the outward fabric and one has, in effect, two jackets in one substance. As his career progressed, Barthes increasingly blurred these distinctions – claiming, indeed (as we shall see in Chapter 4), that they were one and the same.

What is being described in *The Pleasure of the Text*, therefore, is not so much a new mode of criticism as a philosophy of life whose recommendations – an openness to unpredictability and subversion, for instance – are, for the first time in Barthes, *moral* as well as political and critical. This morality is not of a prescriptive kind (one which lays down rules of conduct); it is what is technically known as hedonism: a system based on pleasure as the central value. This pleasure, however, is no utilitarian calculation of yields or consequences. 'Textual' bliss is sudden, inescapable, guiltless and almost impersonal. In it one cannot opt for the estimated greater good, as in utilitarianism, because at the moment of its experience it negates the very self that might calculate such questions. But, lest this seem a cosy belief, one should recall that at the back of it lies Barthes's inevitable pessimism. *The Pleasure of the Text* is a joyful book, written, like *Michelet*, with a sensual attention to complexity and variation which is typical of Barthes's best 'hot' manner.[9] But its foundations lie in the dystopia of the psychoanalytic chains of desire. Bliss is disruptive, elusive and, as ever in Barthes, fugitive: 'to be with the one I love and to think of something else: this is how I have my best ideas . . . ' (*PoT*, 24). Pleasure in Barthes, one might say, is, however immediate, always twinned with pain, and always compensatory.

What is being described by Barthes in books like *S/Z* and *The Pleasure of the Text* is not a methodological criticism. He does not recommend a technique but an attitude, a way of reading which is calculated anachronism. One should, he says, read very slowly: 'not to devour, to gobble, but to graze, to browse scrupulously, to rediscover – in order to read today's writers – the leisure of bygone readings: to be aristocratic readers' (*PoT*, 13). Part of the appeal of his work, therefore, has been that it cuts against the grain of critical approaches which ransack texts for other purposes, like examination answers or politics. Barthes's emphasis on personal pleasure seems to restore something to literature which many feel is lost in critical approaches which downgrade immediate experience, but it is also clear that this has implications which demand discussion.

One of these is clearly put by the structuralist Michael Riffaterre in a review of another of Barthes's books of this period, *Sade/Fourier/Loyola* (1971). Riffaterre argues that Barthes's poststructuralism loses any immediate contact with the literary work itself. 'In effect, [Barthes] defines literary interpretation as fantasy,' writes Riffaterre. 'He sees the literary text not as an intellectual object which he must reflect upon and analyse, but as a language into which he can translate his own existence.' Barthes fails to acknowledge that the vast majority of texts (including many of those which he claims are 'Textual' in his sense) actually 'limit or hierarchize the plurality of meanings'. This is not to say that texts mean only one thing, but to accept that signification is to some degree intentional; it is not a mere matter of arbitrary plurality.[10] In short, Barthes abolishes the difference between himself as a 'Text', and one by Sade, Mallarmé, Keats, or whoever.

This charge is frequently made against poststructuralism. Even critics who were sympathetic towards *S/Z*, like Frank Kermode, were uneasy about subsequent developments.[11] One reason for this is that the idea of 'Text' seems to short-circuit the exchange between literary works and their readers. If '*in the Text, only the reader speaks*' (*S/Z*, 152), then any learning involved in encountering what is new vanishes, because the work is no longer a separate object. Jerome McGann notes the historical consequences of this. If Barthesian 'Text', by definition, happens in the present, it must abolish the past. Not only does this leave us historically ignorant, it forecloses the cognitive activity of reading literature which is, in part, an encounter with the different, historically or otherwise.[12] 'Texts' therefore seem always to tell the same story. In the name of plurality, 'Textuality', in fact, might be said to create a monologue in which the 'Text' enacts the escapades of the reader's subjectivity. Even poststructuralist supporters like Barbara Johnson, author of a fine early essay on *S/Z*, note that *Sarrasine* is made into an allegory of Barthes's own concerns.[13] Sometimes, therefore, poststructuralist criticism is accused of a kind of ventriloquism in which literature plays the dummy.

There are, of course, good defences of Barthes's position (not least the fact that *S/Z* is in truth densely historical). But his work has been part of a wider movement to reconceive the role readers play in the construction of literary meaning, and problems persist in some of these formulations.[14] In *S/Z*, for instance, Barthes declares that 'the writerly Text is a perpetual present' (*S/Z*, 5), and plurality is dependent on forgetting. This is an 'affirmative value' (*S/Z*, 11). But this is exactly what he himself had rejected so strongly only three years previously, in *The Fashion System*, where he deplored incessant innovation in fashion because this ostensible creativity was in fact only repetitious recycling. Even if one puts aside the contradiction, the very least Barthes is implying is an absolute distinction between literature and mass culture, and the writerly reader and the common reader. A number of critics close to Barthes – like Annette Lavers and Pierre Bourdieu – have therefore criticised poststructuralism for its lordly attitudes and class-based definitions of pleasure.[15]

Indeed, the rapid politicisation of 'Textuality' in Britain never really got to grips with the stark contradiction that the tolerant democracy of open 'Textuality' is conducted in Barthes's own account through a manner of reading which he styles 'aristocratic' (*PoT*, 13). Some of Barthes's followers exploit too freely the ambiguities of metaphor in *The Pleasure of the Text* which, as we have seen, instantaneously switches from 'Text' to life. While this helpfully rehumanises literature from the cold grind of structuralism, it also dehumanises the reader in the hot turbulence of 'Textual' forces. Hence, perhaps, some of the thoughtlessly unpleasant language used as small change by some critics in which texts are interrogated, mutilated and dispersed.

One general way of putting these difficulties is to say that in some respects poststructuralism is an idealism. Indeed, the philosopher Richard Rorty has argued that modern 'Textualism' is a late-twentieth-century version of the late-nineteenth-century idealism which influenced literary modernists like T.S. Eliot.[16] The historical argument here is complex, but in some areas of his work Barthes does seem to abandon any notion that 'Text' is shaped by historical or formal elements. As we have seen, he claims that 'Text' is anti-generic, but the generic features of literature are a major source of its effect upon readers, and the same case can be made for the historical elements also. In this sense, 'Text' seems another and extended version of the zero degree, an ultimate of literary performance, though without any attempt on Barthes's part to locate 'Textuality' within the historical framework which was part of the argument of *Writing Degree Zero*, where 'white writing' was an (albeit loose) historical category because it resisted the prevailing dictates of 'Literature'.

'Textuality', however, seems a much more uncertain concept, because Barthes's attention has shifted from the historical to the personal. It is possible to imagine a kind of historical 'Textuality' in which one might study why certain styles flourish in certain periods and are able to give their readers the kind of euphoric experiences in which Barthes is interested. One might go further and ask why it is that certain periods should require their literature to do this while others do not. But this is not what Barthes is interested in. He sometimes seems to want to cut 'Text' adrift from historical and other determinations, and establish it simultaneously as a marginal and a universal fact about language and human psychology. In this sense, Rorty argues, it is like the style of idealist thought which prevailed in late-nineteenth-century Britain.

In fact, Barthes was equivocal about the historicality of 'Text'. Sometimes he speaks as though it is a historical need demanded by modernity (for instance, in the 'Theory of the text' essay); but mainly he writes as though this demand comes from other sources, like 'Texts' themselves or universal psychology. The equivocation is evident in *S/Z* and *The Pleasure of the Text*. According to these books the creation of meaning is an act of 'force' in two senses. There is a political sense which implies that giving meaning to something is an act of violence, a forcible imposition. But there is also a formal sense in which works are composed of forces which shape the reader's comprehension, which is how the codes in *S/Z* are described. However, whereas 'Text' dissolves ideologies and power systems, the codes are forces which 'take over' like imperial invaders (*S/Z*, 21, 97). Barthes thus establishes a dubious series of equations in which any organising structure reiterates the mono-directional rigours of grammar (*S/Z*, 85–6). Thus, he argues, the very notion of orderly form is hierarchically repressive and inti-mately related to the structures of – *inter alia* – the law, the judicial system, capitalist economies and a vaguely conceived 'science'. Narrative, for example, is like merchandise, and involves laws of contract and, therefore, an economic system which regulates the release of meaning (*S/Z*, 88, 152). A related essay, 'Freedom to write' (1976), attacks the 'discriminatory' effects of 'correctness' in spelling, and relishes the productivity of error (*Rustle*, 44–6).

These, of course, are classic shibboleths of 'progressive' educa-tion in the 1960s. What now seems difficult is Barthes's assump-tion that error is innocent. To prize error, one must already possess a cultural competence which is unworried by social or other disadvantage. In Barthes's account error is a plaything, but for many it is hard personal loss and exclusion. So there is a real sense in which the idealism of 'Text' – in this case the separation of error from its social context – is politically problematic. Bar-thes's strong argument, it seems to me, is that 'Textuality' is a vertiginous, blissful loss, but this loss is possible only because one recovers. Error can be profitable in many spheres (like scientific discovery, for instance), but only because it is realised to be so. Barthes's weaker argument is the idealistic assumption that recuperation is incidental; that the loss of hierarchy, structure, meaning, economy, law, grammar and the rest is sufficient.

In *S/Z* Barthes likens the 'Text' to 'a galaxy of signifiers, not a structure of signifieds' (*S/Z*, 5), and later to a 'galaxy of trifling data' (*S/Z*, 22). In between he speaks negatively of the 'nebulae' of meanings which gather to limit the 'Text's' semantic dispersal (*S/Z*, 8). These metaphorical usages are flatly contradictory – not just because astronomical phenomena are used to connote different values without any significant change in the vehicle of the metaphor (is a galaxy preferable to a nebula?), but also because the idea of a galaxy is perhaps inappropriate to Barthes's intended sense. A galaxy suggests mass and abundance; but a galaxy is a structured thing held together by forces, which is the very sense Barthes does not want to give. I would like to think that Barthes intended his metaphorical galaxies to suggest a dialectical sense of form lost and reshaped which would parallel his best arguments about loss and recuperation. And perhaps he did. But there is the suspicion that, in the radicalism of the 'Text', the glamour of the signifier has triumphed over the signs of thought.

In another widespread evocation by metaphor, Barthes makes use of information theory. For him 'Text' is not communication, but static or noise – the jamming, dispersal and interruption of communication (*S/Z*, 9, 131–2, 152). 'Literatures are in fact', he writes, 'arts of noise; what the reader consumes is this defect in communication, this deficient message' (*S/Z*, 145). The idea of noise and the deficient message seems more in tune with the destabilising thrust of his conception of 'Text' than the metaphors of space and mass. But to follow Barthes's thought through, it is necessary to look at this jamming of communication in a more specific context.

Work and play

One argument that is made increasingly is that Barthes's conception of 'Text' is compatible with the new modes of textual production made possible by computers. The argument, though it is complex in operational detail, is simple in outline. Because computer technology can generate multiple overlapping texts, the idea of the intertext has become a material reality. Computer software can place texts side by side, interweave different texts and trace affiliations and connections within seconds. It can realise in quite specific ways the breakdown Barthes sought between the text (in its old sense) and the para-text – that is, the surrounding mesh of commentary and response which literature attracts. Both can be present on the screen at the same time, and the boundaries between text and commentary are now porous. In this way computer-generated text is a *writerly* 'Text' in the Barthesian sense. It can be played with by moving elements around and introducing others as recommended in *The Pleasure of the Text*. The most succinct overview of these developments is George Landow's recent book *Hypertext*. 'Hypertext' is a form of software which achieves all these things, and Landow develops the connection between it and theories of poststructural 'Text'. But hypertext is more complexly related to Barthes's conception of 'Textuality' than is sometimes claimed and this technology is not a latter-day realisation of Barthes's visionary initiative. Technological textuality was conceived contemporaneously with Barthes's bookbound formulation in the technological optimism of the 1960s.

The postwar development of the 'techno-sphere' was particularly pronounced in this period. Advertisements claimed that there were scientific solutions to ancient problems of dirt and feeding, astronomical exploration was a reality, and, in the West, so was cheap travel and personal mobility. Meanwhile, cultural forms were modified by revolutions in cheap printing, innovative design and, especially, the electronic reproduction and amplification of music. All this inevitably changed relationships between individuals and the cultural environment. Cultural productions have a very different mode of existence when they are affordably and transportably popular – something which Barthes glimpsed in *Mythologies*. Mobility of access and the development of telecommunications have changed culture from top to bottom. As a result, many were beginning to rethink the old print-based literary culture which seemed threatened by electronic communications.

In France, Barthes's colleague at *Tel Quel*, Philippe Sollers, claimed in 1965 that the book was now a poor thing, a mere object compared to the sophistication of the 'current information media'.[17] Sollers argued that because communication was now predominantly machine-based, the role of print literature lay in the transgression of communication for the benefit of imaginations threatened by increasing cybernisation. As we saw in Chapter 2, Barthes shared this position, and it became axiomatic on the avant-garde Left. In 1971 Sollers saluted *S/Z* because it recorded the 'crisis in representation itself', and displayed the healthy riot of the 'Textual' imagination.[18] Similarly, in *Of Grammatology* (1967), Jacques Derrida (another *Tel Quel*-ite) argued that modern methods for the storage, retrieval and dissemination of information change ways of thinking about reading:

> The conservation of thought can now be conceived otherwise than in terms of books which will only for a short time keep the advantage of their rapid manageability. A vast 'tape-library' with an electronic selection system will in the near future show pre-selected and instantaneously retrieved information. Reading will still retain its importance for some centuries to come, in spite of its perceptible regression for most men, but writing (understood in the sense of linear inscription) seems likely to disappear rapidly, replaced by automatic dictaphones.[19]

This insight – that the forms of writing are shifting from the linear to the multidimensional – is the material foundation of Derrida's deconstruction, and provides relevant support for the 'hypertext' case.

Perhaps the most influential theorist of this kind in the Anglo-American world was the Canadian Marshall McLuhan. McLuhan's work is now unfashionable, but it has some arresting similarities to that of his French peers. In *The Guttenberg Galaxy* (1962: note the same topical astronomical image as Barthes used in *S/Z*) McLuhan argues that modern culture has freed itself from 'the conditions of passivity' imposed upon it by print-based culture. Print, he argues, inevitably regulates modes of comprehension and insight because of its linearity, its enforced passivity, and the control exerted on it by various forms of cultural clerisy. By contrast, the new technology reawakens readers and makes them more actively productive. Thus the twentieth century will prove to be 'the greatest of all human ages in the arts or the sciences.'[20] The connection between this and the 'Textual' reading Barthes envisages in *S/Z* and *The Pleasure of the Text* is clear. Like Barthes, McLuhan argues for a fundamental reorientation of cultural and textual understanding, and a change in attitude towards the text itself. Instead of ancient reverence, new readers should feel an empowered delight, and McLuhan recommends a 'mosaic or field' approach to culture which resembles Barthes's orientation towards generalised structure. One should no longer think exclusively about the text as 'the words on the page' (as in traditional criticism), but as a component of the general cultural environment. McLuhan's 'mosaic or field' approach establishes the basic grounds of a particular field of understanding rather than focusing narrowly on individual features, while accepting the plurality – the mosaic – of components which constitute any interpretative event.

Understanding Media (1964) develops this ambitious argument. According to this book, the new technology will end conflict and alienation by creating a technologically linked-up global village. At the same time consciousness will change, McLuhan argues, with the technological extension of our sensory and cognitive apparatus, developing 'our central nervous system itself in a global embrace'.[21] McLuhan's is a 'new age' vision; he posits a 'boundary break' in human culture. Newly empowered intellectuals will mediate 'between the old and new power groups' (McLuhan, 47) because 'wholeness, empathy and depth of awareness are a natural adjunct of electric technology' (McLuhan, 13). Like many optimistic visionaries in the 1960s, McLuhan imagines a future society on the model of a work of art. It is an integrated vision of 'ultimate harmony' where the new technology releases leisure and hence, axiomatically, creative contemplation through the wires and beams of the electronic organism. There were many similar visions in the 1960s, though few were quite so enthusiastic for the technological infrastructure. Herbert Marcuse, a Frankfurt Marxist of the 1930s who became an influential guru of the new 'multidimensional man', also argued, in *An Essay on Liberation* (1969), that the developing technology of the cultural environment was transforming the organism itself. For Marcuse this could go two ways: towards a consumer dystopia of manufactured desire similar to that pictured in *The Fashion System*, or towards a utopian release from alienated work and shackled consciousness. Marcuse's optimistic vision called for 'the need for a revolution in perception, for a new sensorium'.[22] Again, the model was the ludic freedom and creative wholeness of art. For Marcuse, as for McLuhan, if technology was to guarantee leisure, then the bulk of life was to be the gamesome, creative realisation of artistic freedom.

This idea runs through much of the radical writing of the period. In Britain, Richard Neville's influential *Play Power* (1970) represents the period's characteristic package of play, pleasure, politics and poetry, and exuberantly tracks down the sources of the revolution in sexual pleasure, narcotics and the various forms of the 'counterculture'. The mix of the bodily, the playful, the personal, the subversive, the hedonistic and the actively expressive is, in general terms, strikingly similar to themes developed by Barthes. Though its idiom and intentions are very different, *Play Power* also adopts a loose fragmented form to celebrate a sensual ludic activism, mixes autobiography with cultural commentary, and frees the 'signifier' in a galaxy of wordplay ('Join the Gentle Strike!'). In the general melting pot of ideas in the late 1960s, these cross-overs are not unexpected. Activists testified to the exhilarating imbroglio of leftist politics, American popular culture and French cultural theory which generated the energy of the period, and it is easy to see the connections between the hedonistic playfulness recommended by the poststructuralists and the (probably rather imaginary) 'Free London' of Neville's cultural 'Underground'.[23] It is also easy to connect the styles adopted there and the signifying practices urged by Barthes and the *Tel Quel* group.

Fashion mixed the proprieties of gender and customary usage in a cultivated outrageousness, and signs were selected for their dysfunctional blankness, like a mixture of Barthes's 'white writing' and the free play of the signifier. The halved-apple logo for Apple, the Beatles' record label, was conceived by its designer as a 'pure symbol', and was never meant to carry any writing (though actually it did); while the Beatles' *White Album* (1968) was released as an empty signifying package without name or title. Similarly, the lyrics, like those of Bob Dylan, made extravagant use of narratives without referential logic and, above all, a density of metaphor which maximised the free play of their signifying potential, as if to follow Barthes's urgings – in an essay on Sollers written in 1965 – 'to set in motion a programme which will open the subject to unheard-of metaphors' (*Sollers*, 45). 'We must use as many metaphors as possible, because metaphor is a means of access to the signifier', he repeated in an interview in 1971 (*Grain*, 115). Fredric Jameson is surely correct to see a connection between this 'stripping-off' of the referent in the theory and practice of writing in the 1960s, and the increasing emphasis being placed on the autonomy of the cultural sphere itself.[24] If leisure and culture were unshackled by the new technologies, then art became the image of an independent utopia.

So in one sense Barthes's ideas of 'Textuality' were companionable forms to other influential ideas of the period. In another way, however, his thinking is not assimilable to its cultural optimism, and his own hostility to the counterculture, and the celebrated Parisian 'events' of May 1968, is well known. In interviews he criticised the counterculture for its 'unintelligent' opposition to traditional culture. The counterculture helped to free certain individuals from cultural silence, and rock music valuably 'expresses a new relation to the body', but as a whole it remained stereotyped. 'Free expression' was not enough, because it was too unselfconscious to resist the lure of derivative stereotypes: 'I see a very great difference', he remarked sententiously, 'between . . . language as expression and language as transformation, as production' (*Grain*, 152). Similarly, the events of May 1968 did not produce change, he argued in 'Writing the event', an essay written in that year, because the revolutionaries and their opponents shared the same symbolic system (*Rustle*, 149–54).

For Barthes, the supposedly free forms of the counterculture only repeated formulae, like routines in the fashion system. New work was 'insufficiently playful' because it did not push powerfully or consciously enough against prevailing norms: 'Culture is a fate to which we are condemned. To engage in radical countercultural activity is therefore simply to move things around, and, unless one is very careful, to rely on the same stereotypes' (*Grain*, 153). The striking thing here is the first sentence. Though he is an opponent of culture in this sense, Barthes is none the less 'condemned' to it, and its rules are necessary for what he calls, in another interview, the 'superior game' (*Grain*, 145). Here we glimpse another of Barthes's paradoxes: he was a cultural iconoclast interested only in culture's 'superior game'.

What distinguishes Barthes from many of his contemporaries, therefore, is the view that the past cannot be shed so easily – that, in McLuhan's terms, the 'boundary break' between the Guttenberg epoch and the electronic epoch is neither abrupt nor inevitable. In a 1971 interview Barthes equivocated when he was asked if he, like Derrida, foresaw 'the end of the book'. He replied that he had an 'apocalyptic' vision not of the end of the book, but of the triumph of 'its most abject forms: the book of mass communications, of consumption, the capitalistic book, in the sense in which a capitalistic society would at that point eliminate all possible play of marginal forms, so that no further cheating and evasion would be possible. And that would be complete barbarism' (*Grain*, 147). Barthes's position here is complex because he is trying to work between two opposed ideas. The first is the view that commercial culture will obliterate imaginative culture. This position could be said to be *the* dominant argument in Anglo-American literary studies from Matthew Arnold onwards. On the other hand, he retains a lively sense that the dominant imaginative culture is in fact complicit with ruling interests. As a result he is left negotiating a tactical position between the roles of defender of high culture and its opponent by arguing that tradition, in itself, is a poor thing, except in so far as it enables its opposite, which cannot exist without it. As a result there is a sometimes strained exchange between the mandarin and the iconoclast in which he cannot settle to either role. Though he finds an intellectual base in the Romantic alienation of the avant-garde, his agnosticism will not allow him to settle into its frozen antagonisms. This, for me, is what makes him an interesting thinker.

In this sense, Barthes is not a utopian writer (though there are other ways of considering this question, as we shall see). In his response to many of the representative radical positions of the 1960s, we see again the powerful streak of political pessimism which runs through his career. For him, there could be no bland elimination of the sociocultural or personal past, and *The Pleasure of the Text* is based on the psychoanalytics of loss. For Barthes, bliss remains always in union with pain, and he (rightly) would have nothing to do with the utopian biology assumed by McLuhan and Marcuse. Their argument (which is essentially a nineteenth-century fallacy) claims that cultural developments change biological structures, and that characteristics acquired in a lifetime can be transmitted to subsequent generations. In reality, culture can only take fortuitous advantage of mutations which thrive in changed cultural conditions. (This is the Darwinian position.) Marcuse and, especially, McLuhan flirt with a technological determinism which argues that technology will determine the evolution of neurological sensibility, and this will grant a greater freedom of creative action. In McLuhan, the argument is moved from the politics of the use and control of technology towards a concentration on the visionary possibilities of technological objects. His social vision – that of the 'global village' – is, meanwhile, a sci-fi version of the 'organic community' of the American New Critics and Leavisites among whom he was trained.[25] Its opposite is the dystopias of *Writing Degree Zero*, *The Fashion System*, Godard's *Alphaville* or *2001: A Space Odyssey*. For Barthes there is no original human creativity or more authentic desire which yearns for a more enabling cultural environment, as both Marcuse and McLuhan imply.[26] Desire and creativity are, as in psychoanalysis, functions of loss: we desire this because we do not have that. For him, 'Text' needs its opposite – the work, the classic, the readerly; the avant-garde requires tradition.

This Janus-faced quality to Barthes's thinking is brilliantly brought out in a recent essay by Katherine Hayles in which she examines his use of modern information theory. She contrasts *S/Z* with the ideas of Claude Shannon, one of the founders of the information theory which grew out of the accelerated interest in electronic communications stimulated by World War II. Shannon worked for the American communications giant AT&T, and tried to improve the economy of information systems by controlling 'noise', the chaotic indeterminacy which wrecks communication but which is endemic to all systems. By contrast, it is this very 'noise' which attracts Barthes and the *Tel Quel* group to literary 'Text'. So there is a symmetry of theory, but a polarity of evaluation. Hayles's point, however, is that though Shannon seems the more conservative, 'both economies appear equally conservative, serving to perpetuate rather than challenge the disciplinary economies in which they are embedded'.[27] Poststructuralist theory is actually highly efficient. It renews scarce resources (the literary canon) by subjecting them to interpretative protocols which have the economic advantage of infinity of meaning. Furthermore, Hayles argues, Barthes oversimplifies information theory by portraying its concerns as mere functionality. In fact, the theory stresses not just efficiency, but the creative manipulation of codes and the role of chance. For modern theorists, information is the realisation of the creative and imaginative possibilities available from chancy environments. Many theorists, therefore, are as opposed to information control as Barthes. But Barthes needs to picture the theory quite otherwise, because 'the economy of his theory requires it' (Hayles, 134). He celebrates the 'repudiation of control in one context' (the theory of the 'Text'), but this is actually 'inseparable from the strategy of gaining control in another', the professionalisation of a new form of literary and cultural analysis (Hayles, 134).

This is a harsh judgement which is perhaps more applicable to Barthes's followers, but it is of a piece with his equivocations on the evaluation of culture, and explains the extraordinarily rapid absorption of poststructuralist theory into the cultural mainstream. As Hayles puts it: 'Derrida and Barthes may be accidents of history, but deconstruction is not' (Hayles, 130). It was, in a sense, required by modern criticism. In *S/Z* she detects an 'equivocation between margin and centre' which represents an 'illusory repudiation of control'. An ostensibly transgressive 'economy of excess' in reality nourishes the disciplinary body (Hayles, 138). It is not, therefore, difficult to see why immediate use can be made of Barthes's ideas of 'Textuality' by modern computer buffs working on the new textual merchandise. 'Hypertext', and other forms of textual software, are a technical (and commercial) realisation of the possibilities of 'Textuality', intertextuality, 'writerly' reading, and the like. But they also defeat Barthes's radical psychological economy of loss ('go-for-it' writing about computers is not prone to a language of loss and difficulty).

In this respect, then, there is no authentic Barthes legacy. His 'Textuality' is a dialectic of acculturation and its other, and as such is representative of the problems of modern cultural radicalism generally, which requires the culture it ostensibly despises for its material and intellectual existence. This is the classic predicament of the avant-garde itself, whose gestures are dependent on the rationalities it offends – which is why avant-garde writing often has an on–off relationship to parody; and why, for me, much of Philippe Sollers's writing, for instance, reads like Tony Hancock's parody of bohemian poetry in *The Poetry Society* (1959): 'that's it sunder flounder your death coma grossly inverted placenta cancer aureola from where i sit i see them drip drop by drop bazooka . . .' (It is difficult to know where to stop the quotation.)[28]

In 'From work to text' (1971) Barthes makes the important point that 'The theory of the Text can only coincide with a practice of writing' (*IMT*, 164). The writing most vividly before Barthes himself in this period was the *Tel Quel* avant-garde, but it is important to recognise a general artistic concern. Contemporary

writing is increasingly preoccupied by textual questions of a Barthesian kind, as writers need both to use and to resist a language
which carries inevitable connections with cultural power and authority. This kind of situation is particularly prevalent in colonial or
post-colonial writing in English from Africa, the Caribbean or
Ireland, for instance, and indeed from literary 'subgroups' within
Britain itself. Writing by women, for example, often exists in
difficult torsion with mainstream forms. The ubiquity of this
problem is part of the difficulty of finding satisfactory illustration
of Barthesian 'Textuality', because we are dealing with a critical
method which may perhaps only be exemplified as practice. This
section will therefore close with work that is companionable to the
the tragic modes of loss, the radical face of Barthes's theoretical
Janus. I have in mind the recent work of the contemporary British
dramatist Howard Barker.

   This book focuses only incidentally on Barthes's interest in the
theatre, though this was one of his major preoccupations in the
early part of his career, and the example of Brecht remained an
abiding influence. There is no space to develop this aspect of
Barthes's work here (Michael Moriarty's book on Barthes, listed in
the Bibliography, covers the ground expertly), but it is important
to realise the role theatrical conceptions play in developing the
'Textual' model. In the 1971 'Avant-Propos' to *Essais Critiques*, for
instance (which is not translated in the English edition), he laments the neglect of Brecht by the contemporary avant-garde, and
a related essay, 'Brecht and discourse' (1975), characterises Brecht
as an intensely dialectical writer. Brecht has no 'message'. Instead,
his theatre is one of 'fragments' and loss, a deliciously stylised,
sensuous 'noise' which leaves the spectator without security
(*Rustle*, 212–22). In Barthes's search for alternative metaphors for
the 'Text', this seemed a helpful analogue, and increasingly the
theatre represents for him an image of the way discourses or
subjectivities are displayed *in conflict*.

   In *S/Z* he writes of the way 'Text' avoids the static frames of
pictures, or the revelations of narrative dénouements, and instead
shares the multiplicity and unresolved developments of Brechtian
theatre (*S/Z*, 55–6, 187). In 'Theory of the text', the 'Text' is 'the
very theatre of a production where the producer and reader meet'
('Theory', 36). In *Sade/Fourier/Loyola* (1971) he writes of a '*the-
atricalization*' of language which is not 'designing a setting for

representation, but unlimiting the language' (*SFL*, 6). The image also runs throughout his later books, *Roland Barthes by Roland Barthes* and *A Lover's Discourse*; and, commenting on *Sade/Fourier/Loyola*, Barthes remarks: 'I attempt to dissipate or elude the moral discourse that has been held on each of them . . . I unglue the text from its purpose as a guarantee: socialism, faith, evil' (*SFL*, 9) – his explicit model, once again, is Brecht. It therefore seems apt to look to another dramatist in order to examine Barthes's 'Textuality' a little further.

Howard Barker's work has never been comfortably assimilated to that of the generation of British socialist dramatists with whom he is usually classed. Though he has called himself a socialist, his politics – like Barthes's – are difficult to determine with much precision, and recent theoretical manifestos suggest drama of quite a different kind. These statements strikingly resemble the ethos and direction of radical poststructuralism. Barker, too, is an enemy of humanism. In an interview in 1980 he attacked the liberal-humanist consensus: 'I certainly don't intend to aim for more "maturity", "fair-mindedness" or any other of the weary baggage of critical humanism. . . . It's death in drama.' He describes his politics as uncertain: 'It is easy to say you are a revolutionary socialist, but it is stale with cliché and a certain vanity. I knew that then, as now, I believed revolution necessary but unlikely. That tension is at the hub of my work.'[29] Since then he has written about the 'extinction of official socialism', and concluded that 'when the opposition loses its politics, it must root in art'.[30] This, of course, is congruent with the position Barthes developed in the early 1970s. Like Barthes's 'Text', Barker's theatre – which he describes variously as 'tragic theatre', 'catastrophism' or the 'theatre of loss' – is concerned with the same vertiginous erosion of the conventional self which is a speciality of 'Text'. The dynamic interaction between audience and play in Barker's work mirrors pretty exactly that between reader and 'Text' in Barthes, whose influence, as far as I am aware, Barker does not claim. Barker cultivates an oxymoronic, dialectical view of drama – 'The triumph in defeat' – which resembles Barthes's version of Brecht.[31] It is to be found in recent plays, principally *The Possibilities* (1988), *The Last Supper* (1988) and *Seven Lears* (1989).

Barker's argument assumes collapse and disintegration. This is both a condition and a desideratum. The condition is provided by the deterioration of the ethical and social policy consensus of the 1960s and, with it, the humanistic moral community. While this lasted, Barker argues, it enabled a 'common ethical ground among artist, actor and audience' and 'the two sacred groves of contemporary theatre – clarity and realism' ('The triumph in defeat'). Their collapse means that a new theatre is needed and enabled, but this new practice cannot repair a damaged culture with new maxims and rallying points. Rather, theatre should reflect its ruin. Most of his plays, therefore, create smashed and savage mental and physical landscapes; and the acceptance of disintegration, he argues, shifts the ground of ethical argument decisively from arguments *on* the stage to arguments *between* stage and audience ('The triumph in defeat'). If there is no ethical language worth having, obviously there is none worth speaking. The new ethical practice, therefore, needs to be transactional, not expressive.

However, because Barker believes there is no available public language, the theatre of tragic catastrophism, like the 'negativity' of literary language in Barthes or Kristeva, revels in the destruction of the sham of consensus, which is why collapse is a desideratum. Ethical action, for Barker, can base itself only on 'disruption', 'instability' and 'loss' – the kind of experience which tragedy used to make available. This loss, he argues in 'Understanding exits', is in turn a release of the imaginative, the unconscious and the visionary from the shackles of orthodox narrative, naturalistic language (which, 'thin on metaphor, annihilates ambiguity') and the oppressive presence of tidy meaning. Thus the new theatre, through transgression, liberates its audience from the tyranny of 'understanding', and opens it to the possibilities of the perverse and the contradictory to combat banality and triviality ('49 asides'). In this it shares the radical scepticism and suspicion of communal discourses to be found in much poststructuralism. Barker is also, like Barthes, prone to speak in the language of ecstatic sexuality to convey this process of creative tension and loss. It is a freeing from shame and guilt as well as from an imprisoning rationality. Thus both poststructuralism and catastrophe theatre celebrate the literary as disruptive plurality and 'chaos'. The powerful strand of imagery in *S/Z* which emphasises collapse is realised on Barker's stages.

Barker's aesthetics are, like Barthes's, anti-referential. In the programme-text to *The Last Supper* he writes:

I gnawed at English socialism for ten years, from *Claw*, through *A Passion in Six Days*, to *Downchild*, coming at last to History, which is where I had begun [Barker studied History at university], neither official history nor documentary history, whose truth I deny, but the history of emotion, looking for a politics of the emotions. I discovered that the only things worth describing now are things that do not happen, just as the only history plays worth writing concern themselves with what did not happen. New writing began at the Royal Court with the description of things that were seen (i.e. real life). Writing now has to engage with what is not seen (i.e. the imagination) because real life is annexed, reproduced, soporific.[32]

As in much poststructuralism, there is a delight in paradox (the history of what has not happened) and the collapse of referential history into discourse. Relatedly, everyday life is thought to be routinised and damaging – a view that comes from the same late-1960s ideas which sponsored Barthes's libertarian 'Textual' hedonism. (Barker insists on the European dimensions of his concerns and is published by John Calder, traditionally Britain's leading publisher of the European and transatlantic avant-garde.) Barker's drama develops through the manipulation of mythic and literary materials. The literary bearings of *Seven Lears* are obvious, and clearly *The Last Supper* (subtitled 'A New Testament') draws on Christian myth, painterly and literary conceptions of this subject, and classical notions of the writer's role (the hapless poet in it is called Apollo). This is interleaved with references to the recent history of Eastern Europe and a sardonic glancing account of postwar British Labourism (the soldiery are called McAttlee, McStain and McNoy).

Barker, therefore, is a vigorously deconstructive and intertextual writer. His characters, and their spectators, wander among war, empire and ruin. Alienated from orthodoxy, betrayed by institutions, politically baffled and denied the consolations of nature in our dirty twentieth-century greenhouse, they seek solace in the imagination and the force of human desire. Thus the characters in *The Last Supper* stare yearningly from a window like their intertextual fellows in Beckett's *Endgame*, while the imaginations of Barker's audience stroll across stages peopled by victims of catastrophes, political and ecological, happened, happening or to come.

Barker's theoretical position, like his theatrical language, seems to me very original in British theatre at present. The general shape and tendency of his arguments, however, are of a piece with wider shifts in the ways in which we think about art. The abrasive relationship between the literary work and its audience reflects a sustained ambiguity about culture in both Barker and Barthes. The emphasis on loss, and the collapse of the shared language of a valuable ethical and political community, reiterates a leading theme of modernism, and reflects the writer's social alienation, which Barthes took as axiomatic. The consequences of this for criticism are complex but, as a general movement of thought, there is a powerful momentum towards the privatisation of experience.

Traditional Anglo-American criticism has tended, on the whole, to insist that valuable aesthetic properties have immediate collective advantages. The formal balance which I.A. Richards and the New Critics felt necessary for good poems because it promoted psychological and social equilibrium, the 'felt life' and moral engagement which Leavis made a criterion for membership of the 'Great Tradition', the effort to bring together the personal and collective in Doris Lessing or Raymond Williams's defence of realism, are belligerently opposed in Barthes and Barker alike. There are, of course, good reasons for this, but it is interesting that the radical individualism of 'Text' has been so easily recouped without loss in the technological professionalisation of computer text and the efficient capitalisation of the stray products of information 'noise'. In the next phase of Barthes's career, he begins to explore the consequences of this individualism more fully, and his next books drift from the 'Text' to the dynamics of the self who experiences a social world of mutual need as well as blissful release. Barthes's work remains individualistic in orientation, but his last books begin to revise the ideas of his poststructuralist period.

Selves and lovers:
late Barthes

The book of the self

This chapter will examine the final stage of Barthes's career, from
his work on 'Textuality' to his death in 1980. It comprises three
books – *Roland Barthes by Roland Barthes* (1975), *A Lover's Discourse* (1977) and *Camera Lucida* (1980) – but, as with any career,
it does not separate neatly from earlier interests. Indeed, we have
already remarked that the concern with the self which dominates
this period follows from *S/Z* and *The Pleasure of the Text* in
picturing the self in unstable crisis. But these three late texts also
break from this conception of language and 'Textuality'. In *Roland
Barthes*, Barthes emphasises that his work develops by the displacement of earlier priorities: the 'Text' displaced structuralism,
'But again the Text risks paralysis: it repeats itself, counterfeits
itself in lusterless texts, testimonies to demand for readers, not for
a desire to please: the Text tends to degenerate into Prattle (*Babil*).
Where to go next? That is where I am now' (*RB*, 71). Barthes had
exhausted the idea. The essay, which had been his most accomplished mode since the mid-1950s, is now replaced with a more
adventurous fictionality: 'Doom of the essay, compared to the
novel,' he remarks in *Roland Barthes*: 'doomed to *authenticity* – to
the preclusion of quotation marks' (*RB*, 89). This interest in

fictionality in *Roland Barthes* and *A Lover's Discourse* leads, in *Camera Lucida*, to a rejection of the poststructuralist positions which were his most immediate legacy in Anglo-American theory.

In *S/Z* Barthes makes two key assumptions about the self. The first is that 'The "I" which approaches the text is already itself a plurality of other texts, of codes which are infinite or, more precisely, lost (whose origin is lost)' (*S/Z*, 10). The second is that this already textual self is, classically, a system of authority. This argument has two forms: that classic texts assert truth claims, and that classic subjectivities are in thrall to the authorities that compose them. By contrast, modern texts and modern selves are – at least temporarily in the 'Text' of bliss – free from these determinations:

> In modern texts, the voices are so treated that any reference is impossible: the discourse, or better, the language, speaks: nothing more. By contrast, in the classic text the majority of the utterances are assigned an origin, we can identify their parentage . . . either a consciousness (of a character, of an author) or a culture (the anonymous is still an origin, a voice . . .): however, it may happen that in the classic text, always haunted by the appropriation of speech, the voice gets lost, as though it had leaked out through a hole in the discourse. (*S/Z*, 41)

In classic writing, therefore, both the text and the self are subject to a battering of discourses which construct their identity. The modern self, on the other hand, is imaged by multiplicity, gaps and hidden dimensions – a network of strings and holes through which language plays (*S/Z*, 20). It is 'a polyhedron faceted by the word' (*S/Z*, 14). This image is especially interesting. In *Principles of Literary Criticism* (1924), I.A. Richards's classic statement of many of the founding assumptions of Anglo-American 'New Criticism', he compares the ideal action of the mind to the balancing of a similar polyhedron. Literary works nourish this poise as the various signifying forces establish an equilibrium among themselves, and the 'health of the mind' is maintained.[1] In Barthes's metaphor, by contrast, the modern text opens up the many-sided signifying options behind each sign, and the stable self is subverted. The difference between the two usages illustrates the difference between the two conceptions of the ideal self in the two critical traditions.

The idea of the self as constituted by a plurality of 'voices' is not, however, unique to Barthes, or to French poststructuralism.

In *A Portrait of the Artist as a Young Man* (1916) James Joyce uses the same idea:

> While his mind had been pursuing its intangible phantoms and turning in irresolution from such pursuit he heard about him the constant voices of his father and of his masters urging him to be a good catholic above all things. These voices had now become hollowsounding in his ears. When the gymnasium had opened he had heard another voice urging him to be strong and manly and healthy and when the movement towards national revival had begun to be felt in the college yet another voice had bidden him to be true to his country and help to raise up her language and tradition. In the profane world, as he foresaw, a worldly voice would bid him raise up his father's fallen state by his labours and, meanwhile, the voice of his school comrades urged him to be a decent fellow . . . It was the din of all these hollowsounding voices that made him halt irresolutely in pursuit of phantoms.[2]

Indeed, it is possible to read Joyce's novel as an example of the ways in which the self is constructed under the pressures of diverse languages.[3] This idea sometimes seems ubiquitous, and modern writers frequently represent the relationship of individuals to culture as a relationship between desire and the forms in which this desire might be expressed. In *The Magic Toyshop* (1967), Angela Carter makes fruitful use of intertextual reference to tell the story of a young girl's passage through adolescence in a patriarchal environment. The opening pages describe her 'posed in attitudes' before a mirror as she recapitulates a history of modern sexual display of women from the Pre-Raphaelites, through Toulouse Lautrec and *Lady Chatterley's Lover*, to modern film starlets at Cannes. Carter's point is that her heroine's sexuality develops within cultural images which, though ostensibly transgressive, remain male. In posing herself in this way, Melanie constructs her selfhood on the basis of watching herself as an imaginary being, and her most intimate self is forming as an *imago* derived from outside. The remainder of the novel is then concerned to work through this problem.

Our own experience usually presents itself as coherent and 'truthful': that is, we are conscious that we sometimes fantasise or are wrong, but by and large we think we understand our own history clearly enough. But, as the example above makes clear, in poststructuralist argument the personal, the cultural, the imaginary and the ideological are much more tightly woven than we ordinarily suspect. For Carter, as for Barthes, therefore, one important function of fiction is that it is able to dramatise these relationships by playing between the reader's subjectivity, which can recognise these processes, and the subjectivity represented in the fiction, which does not. Readers have the experience of both similarity and difference in a way denied, for example, to Melanie, before her mirror in *The Magic Toyshop*, who is 'living' the experiences which form her. This theme preoccupied Barthes in his last decade, and it is at once apparent that it represents a significant development beyond the theory of 'Textuality' formulated in the early 1970s. The blissful release found in 'Text' is a non-reflective experience: it can be described, as Barthes says, only by metaphor. The commentary on 'Text' therefore travels with the experience itself, but what Barthes is now seeking to understand is a much more wide-ranging conception of the psychological life. If his dominant metaphor for 'Textual' bliss was the explosion, his new metaphor is a much more traditional conception of the mind as an unrolling fabric, albeit one cut into fantastic patterns.

At the same time Barthes preserves the scepticism of poststructural theories of knowledge. There are two arguments here. First, there can be no single, truthful language. In the poststructural world it is the 'play' of language which constitutes the world's reality; and in some extreme versions, the reason why some discourses are seen to be truer than others is only a matter of social power and status. The second argument concerns representation. If Barthes is to deal with a mental world which is a complex meshing of different discursive forces – in an interview he speaks of the 'different wavelengths' of subjectivity (*Grain*, 301) – there is no theoretical language which will 'translate' this adequately into stable conceptual terms. Thus Barthes's language needs to change, and the most immediately striking thing about *Roland Barthes* and *A Lover's Discourse* is their unusual formal organisation. We will come to this in more detail shortly, but Barthes is intellectually consistent in this respect.

If he abandons the 'authentic' discourse of the essay (because there can be no such thing as a sole authentic discourse in this sense), then what is happening in these late books is an exploration of the fictionality of *all* languages, including those of criticism, psychology, politics, and so on. But the notion of fictionality here is a complex one, and Barthes does not mean the convention which opposes truth to fiction. Instead, he is describing a familiar world in which 'the truth' as such cannot appear. We are thoroughly accustomed to scepticism about news reports, official announcements, and so on, and we have all suspected an account of events without knowing the 'real' state of affairs. This situation – sometimes rather grandly called the 'hermeneutics of suspicion' in modern theory – is Barthes's terrain in his late work. It is not truth which frees us from ideology, he claims in *Roland Barthes*, but fiction: 'counter-ideology creeps in by means of a fiction' (*RB*, 104). But his exact way of putting it is important. This is a world of 'creeping-in' and tactical usage; it is not an opposition of truth to ideology. In late Barthes, fiction is a positive term because it is liberated from the need for ultimate authenticity.

Poststructuralist argument has pursued these ideas in different areas, but Barthes's topic is the personal – or, more precisely, that intersection of the personal and the public which we call the self or subjectivity. Of the three last books one, *Roland Barthes*, is a highly eccentric form of autobiography, and the other two mingle an 'objective' topic – the language and behaviour of lovers in *A Lover's Discourse*, photography in *Camera Lucida* – with the personal and subjective. Again the method is coherent. In *S/Z* Barthes had briefly tried to reconceptualise the relationship between subjective and objective not as stable positions (the subjective here, the truth over there) but as 'forces' which ebb and flow around any given event. What we accept as truthful or 'objective' is often merely the stereotype we take for granted; and, as ever in Barthes, nothing is to be taken for granted (*S/Z*, 10). In his late work, as in *Mythologies*, the stereotype is where 'reality' congeals and coats the world with its thoughtless glue. So the form of these late works resists convention.

Roland Barthes is the best example. The book was written in the same series as Barthes's book on Michelet, the introductory 'Écrivains de toujours', so it has the context of an academic textbook. Barthes preserves the easily digested sectional divisions, the illustrations, the chronology, and so forth, but radically redistributes them to dismantle the convention. Thus *Roland Barthes by Roland Barthes* starts with forty-odd pages of pictures with cryptic commentaries in the manner of a caption. The writing gets under way only when Barthes begins his intellectual maturity, so the pictures are a way of 'representing' the early part of his life 'pre-intellectually'. The remainder of the book is then organised as a series of *pensées* which reflect backwards and forwards on his career. These fragments are presented in a arbitary way (as in *A Lover's Discourse*, the order is roughly alphabetical). Sometimes a handful will follow through a line of thinking over two or three pages, but mainly the effect is deliberately haphazard and is, again, reminiscent of elliptical modernist forms like Joyce's *Portrait of the Artist*.

Barthes's rationale is careful. He is aiming at a mode of writing which he described as novelistic montage (*Grain*, 285). The purpose is partly to image the way in which memory works (looking back at our lives we remember moments, and coherent patterns are often retrospectively imposed) and partly to make clear Barthes's belief that the personality itself is fragmented, not an integrated 'whole'. Partly, also, the form enacts a desirably relaxed plurality (*RB*, 77). As Alain Robbe-Grillet, Barthes's long-time ally, put it in an obituary tribute, 'the Barthesian fragment shifts [*glisse*] continuously and its meaning is situated not in the bits of content that will appear here and there, but, on the contrary, *in the shifting [glissement] itself.*'[4] Barthes says as much in *Roland Barthes*. Speaking of metaphor, he comments that the point of metaphor is not what is revealed by it but the actual act of displacement, of shifting the language: 'the meaning transferred matters little or nothing, the terms of the trajectory matter little or nothing: the only thing that counts – and establishes metaphor – is *the transference itself*' (*RB*, 123). So *Roland Barthes* is a *performance* in language as much as a representation, and this is why Barthes looks increasingly to a non-discursive metaphoric register: to visual art, music and images of dysfunctional objects.

In *Roland Barthes*, there are images of radios which cannot be tuned (*RB*, 74), inventive piano players who become machines (RB, 70), and telephones which fade (*RB*, 86). All illustrate that understanding is incomplete or faulty. In *A Lover's Discourse* the same dysfunctional telephone appears again (*LD*, 114–15), and Barthes adds scratched records (*LD*, 21), and glues that will not bond. At the same time another set of images stresses plurality, superimpositions, reflections, mirages or cockeyedness: things never seem quite to *work* in Barthes's world. There is a chaos of redundant objects; nothing aligns properly or sits flush; everything is a matter of edges. There is no consistency: everything moves about, grows or decomposes. It is a febrile, refractory, knockabout world, and it is no accident that *Roland Barthes* praises great comedians: Chaplin offers a 'complete kind of joy' because he provides an image of the differential and the plural (*RB*, 54); and the Marx Brothers' *A Night at the Opera* provides an allegory of 'the wild mechanics of the text-on-a-spree':

> the steamer cabin, the torn contract, the final chaos of the opera doors – each of these episodes (among others) is the emblem of the logical subversions performed by the Text; and if these emblems are perfect, it is ultimately because they are comic, laughter being what, by a last reversal, releases demonstration from its demonstrative attribute. What liberates metaphor, symbol, emblem from poetic *mania*, what manifests its power of subversion, is the preposterous . . . The logical future of metaphor would therefore be the gag. (*RB*, 80–1)

Often Barthes's pessimism gives his work the feel of tragedy. But *Roland Barthes* and *A Lover's Discourse* (though not *Camera Lucida*) are also *farcical* texts, deploying comic examples, embarrassment and the ridiculous to celebrate a playful transformation which is analogous to the quirky adventures of language itself. Elsewhere in *Roland Barthes*, he writes that he relishes the adage of Marx (Karl this time) that sometimes history recurs as farce. He enjoys it because – like metaphor – it exploits the ambiguous instability of things as they become fiction, alter qualities and, like a comedian, 'lean, fade and fall' (*RB*, 88–9). In this respect the last texts resemble *Michelet* and *Mythologies* in their fecund ingenuity, which exploits the play between the potential disaster (the fragmented self, the suicidal lover, the ideological historian, the consumer dystopia) and the inherent quirky insobriety of things-in-themselves. Like *Mythologies*, *Roland Barthes* deploys the mock-heroic and alerts readers to his own inconsistences, hypocrisies and a poor body plagued by headaches and mild sensualities: 'my body is not a hero', he remarks mournfully (*RB*, 60).

Roland Barthes, then, unsettles its generic format at diverse levels. It courts fictionality, comedy and the self-delightingly gratuitous ('To begin with, some images: they are the author's treat to himself, for finishing his book . . . ' *RB*, 3). It is also written in an eccentric syntax which creates the effect of thought-in-process, a kind of stream-of-intellection. Here is an example:

one borrows from science certain conceptual procedures, an energy of classification: one steals a language, though without wishing to apply it to the end: impossible to say: this is denotation, this connotation, or: this passage is readerly, this writerly, etc.: the opposition is *struck* (like a coinage), but one does not seek to *honour* it. Then what good is it? Quite simply, it serves *to say something*: it is necessary to posit a paradigm in order to produce a meaning and then to be able to divert it, to alter it. (*RB*, 92)

The syntax, the punctuation (which will not allow the sentence to end: it is the same in the French), the repeated rhythmical clauses, the questioning, the play between this and the emphatic italics, the disconcerting metaphor and scandalous vocabulary ('stealing', 'not honouring' – the section is called 'Forgery') – all these not only mime the act of thought itself moving through its processes, but also enact its argument: that 'scientific' language is merely a conventional codification of information, it has only 'pretensions to law' (*RB*, 160). While Barthes accepts its efficacy ('one borrows' from it), he will not accept that it displays the world in anything like a satisfactory form. At its most polemical *Roland Barthes* attacks the process of reasoning itself as merely the action of solidified metaphors, a view he derived from Nietzsche (*RB*, 152). But at the same time Barthes borrows science's intellectual energy, makes a rhetoric from it, and demands a new 'enormous science' of subjectivity (*RB*, 79). Once again, this is a calculated textual instability backed by a hard-headed intellectual position. As he says in the quotation above, 'it is necessary to posit a paradigm in order to produce a meaning'.

The difficulties with this position are very evident: inconsistency, unscrupulousness, and a refusal to think about the very real (and not merely discursive) referentiality of empirical science are but three. But the position also has advantages. For instance, Barthes develops the argument that self-consciousness in language helps the development of new work into a moral position (*RB*, 66). For him, assertive arguments are *violent* arguments: they impose upon others, often covertly (as in ideology). So an intellectual style which is able to cope with conflict by accommodating antinomies is ethically valuable. In *Roland Barthes*, Barthes calls this 'The Neutral', and he connects it both to his old notion of 'white writing' and to Zen philosophy, in which he was beginning to be increasingly interested. The Neutral is a way of short-circuiting binary conflicts (active–passive, subjective–objective, mind–body, and so on), and is related to a number of other cognate ideas in the book: 'ease' (the 'ethical force' of the loss of heroism, *RB*, 44), the struggle to write without assertion, 'drifting' (the resistance to intellectual 'pigeonholing', *RB*, 49), and the dispersal of the self into plurality. The Neutral, however, does not transcend conflict; it is 'not the third term – the zero degree – of an opposition . . . it is . . . the second term of a new paradigm, of which violence . . . is the primary term' (*RB*, 132–3). Conflict is the condition which enables its ethical opposite to appear. Thus, when Barthes describes moral activity, he uses a language inflected by violence and sexuality. Morality is born, he writes, when:

> the (abhorred) illusion of the *self-evident* chips, cracks, the machine of languages starts up, 'Nature' shudders with all the sociality compressed within it . . . meaning, before collapsing into insignificance, shudders still . . . it remains fluid, shuddering with a faint ebullition . . . an enormous and perpetual rustling animates with countless meanings which explode, crepitate, burst-out without ever assuming the definitive form of a sign grimly weighted by its signified. (*RB*, 97–8)

This is the language of cataclysm, not easement. Ethics in Barthes are not passive, and gentleness – a categorical Barthesian virtue, repeatedly stressed – is dialectical.

One of the advantages of 'fictional' language is that it plays off the categorical against the performative, and *Roland Barthes* does this repeatedly. Assertions about value are regularly couched in disruptive language, dramatising the plurality which is both an organising principle and ethically desirable. In this 'book of the Self' (*RB*, 119), in which 'It must all be considered as if spoken by a character in a novel' (*RB*, 1), there is no existential surety. The self is a dramatic sequence, not an 'authentic' unity (*RB*, 56). There is no room for the epiphany or 'spot of time' which often organises autobiographical writing. In this way *Roland Barthes* is a deadpan surface without significant highlights. In the middle, Barthes has a section entitled 'Pause: anamneses'. Anamneses are recollections of time past, but the point about Barthes's fifteen snippets of memory is their banality and insignificance, their resistance to the customary expectations of autobiographical writing. The point about the drama of Barthes's self in *Roland Barthes* is often the absence of drama.

The notion that the self is essentially dramatic and existentially ungrounded is a common modern idea. In an interview in 1977, Barthes claims Nietzsche as a source, in particular 'what Nietzsche tells us about the need to "dramatize", to adopt a method of "dramatization" – which for me had the epistemological advantage of prying me away from the metalanguage' (*Grain*, 284). The Anglo-American tradition is also familiar with such ideas in sociology from, for instance, Erving Goffman's *The Presentation of Self in Everyday Life* (1956), or the psychology of 'encounter' theory, or the 'transactional analysis' of Eric Berne's immensely popular *Games People Play* (1964), or existential ideas such as those embedded in R.D. Laing's *Knots* (1970). In literature the idea runs (obviously enough) through much contemporary drama, and Harold Pinter's plays manipulate several 'Barthesian' themes: the aggressivity of language, the fictionality of the self, and the irreconcilable contestation of ideas of truth.

But in *Roland Barthes* it is, once again, Brecht who provides Barthes's model for the self conceived under these modern conditions. Brecht's work is the model for the way fiction contests ideology (*RB*, 104), for the way in which subversion can be delicate, and not confrontational (*RB*, 107), and for writing about politics which does not neglect the aesthetic (*RB*, 53–4). In particular Brecht's theory of acting influenced Barthes's conception of autobiography. Brecht believed that actors should preserve a distance from the character to allow the audience to see beyond individual personality. This idea lies behind Barthes's alternation between the first- and third-person pronouns in *Roland Barthes*. By 'speaking of himself in the manner of the Brechtian actor who must distance his character' (*RB*, 168), Barthes is able to manipulate perceptions to avoid the self settling into one frame of reference. The effect produced is the same riddling alternation of perspective which Laing used in *Knots*, and which also became a feature of some French feminist poststructuralist writing by Kristeva, Hélène Cixous, and others. Barthes writes: '*I would be nothing if I did not write. Yet I am elsewhere than where I am when I write. I am worth more than what I write.*' (*RB*, 169). The effect of these syntactical and referential contortions is endemic to the theatrical metaphor. The idea of the self as performance provides perspectival permutations on ways of seeing in which the self is both the actor performing a role (and therefore conscious of two selves simultaneously) and the spectator observing the actor performing the role, et cetera.

But this dramatising, friable self also has a dark side which Barthes registers only obliquely. The notion of the fragmented self was also becoming increasingly widely used in the study of mental illness. It formed the cornerstone of descriptions of schizoid states in R.D. Laing's influential *The Divided Self* (1960), and it features surprisingly frequently in Anglo-American literature of the period. Pinter's *The Caretaker* (1960), the poems of Sylvia Plath, novels by Plath, Doris Lessing, Jean Rhys and Ken Kesey are a few examples. It also played a major part in French intellectual debate, and Barthes could not have been other than conscious of it. The French-Martinican, Frantz Fanon, working in Algeria, described schizophrenia as one of the psychological legacies of colonialism in *Black Skin, White Masks* (1952), and his ideas were energetically publicised by Sartre, who wrote the preface to Fanon's best-known book, *The Wretched of the Earth* (1965).

More important still, however, was Foucault's pioneering *Madness and Civilisation* (1961). This was published, in a partial translation, in Britain in 1965 in a series edited by Laing, and an important bridge was established between the British 'anti-psychiatry' movement developed by Laing (who was himself much influenced by Sartre) and Foucault's critique of the diagnostic categories used to define mental illness. Both sets of work, and related endeavours like those of Thomas Szasz in America, tried to rescue 'the mad' from medical marginalisation and incomprehension, and attacked the regimes of medical, legal and institutional power which, it was argued, exacerbated the condition.

In France, Foucault maintained the argument in a high-profile campaign throughout the 1970s against institutionalised power in all sectors of public life (the clinic, the prison, the penal code), and radical Lacanians like Gilles Deleuze and Félix Guattari pushed the anti-psychiatry arguments still further. Their *Anti-Oedipus: Capitalism and Schizophrenia* (1972) rejected Laing on the grounds that he retained a residual sense of the normative 'whole person'. By contrast, they brutally argued that human beings under capitalism were no more than interchangeable machine-parts. In this context the fragmenting of the personality in schizophrenia was seen not only as a legitimate, utopian protest against capitalist rationality, but also as a more authentic condition of the self.[5]

So the idea of the splintered, schizoid self was well established by the time Barthes wrote *Roland Barthes*, and one of the biggest problems is the book's valorisation of the fragmented self which draws on the spurious glamour attached to mental illness in radical and avant-garde circles. Radicals were quick to make connections between what was taken to be the normalisation of alienation in capitalist culture and the schizoid conditions which resulted. This coincided with an overestimation of irrationality (in drug experiences, for instance), which was seen as a positive benefit. The result was a foolish theoretical glorification of madness which was far removed from the pain evident in the case histories and literary works mentioned above.[6] *Roland Barthes* and other works stress the energising rapture of the fragmented self, but in *The Divided Self* Laing actually paints a different picture. Barthes abandons the authenticating but 'exhausting pursuit of an old piece of myself' with a joke: 'I do not try to *restore* myself (as we say of a monument)' (*RB*, 56). But this joke works only because the self is not in pieces to the degree some of the rhetoric of *Roland Barthes* or *The Pleasure of the Text* might suggest. Laing's simple point is that in schizoid individuals 'we cannot give an adequate account of the existential splits unless we can begin from the concept of a unitary whole, and no such concept exists'.[7] Formally, no such concept exists in *Roland Barthes* either, but actually it is the psychological entity which holds the discourse together.

Barthes recognises this intermittently. He remarks that the 'aphoristic tone of the book' is actually of a piece with the 'classical' conception of the essential self the book sets itself to undermine, and Barthes knowingly draws upon the particularly French tradition of apothegmatic, self-mutating autobiographical reflection in writers such as Montaigne, Pascal and Le Rochefoucauld. The tone, the command, the peremptory generalisations, all suggest a self in lordly command of its intellectual and psychological environment. 'Why then not reject it?' Barthes asks. 'The reason is, as always, emotive: I write maxims (or I sketch their movement) *in order to reassure myself*: when some disturbance arises, I attenuate it by confiding myself to a fixity which exceeds my powers' (*RB*, 179). Similarly, he writes: 'I have the illusion to suppose that by breaking up my discourse I cease to discourse in terms of the imaginary about myself.' But because the fragment is '*finally* a rhetorical genre . . . by supposing I disperse myself I merely return, quite docilely, to the bed of the imaginary' (*RB*, 95). 'The imaginary' has a specialised sense which we will explore in the next section, but Barthes is being very honest here. The tactics of the 'dispersed self' are, in fact, a literary game in which the valorisation of fragmentation is an argumentative and rhetorical counter in the long battle with stereotype. But the generalisations Barthes makes have more dubious effects and values.

At one point Barthes wonders how a book of fragments can ever end because any organising principle must, by definition, be absent:

> Having uttered the substance of these fragments for some months, what happens to me subsequently is arranged quite spontaneously (without forcing) under the utterances that have already been made: the structure is gradually woven, and in creating itself, it increasingly magnetizes: thus it constructs for itself, without any plan on my part, a repertoire that is both finite and perpetual, like that of language. (*RB*, 162)

This is a perfectly responsible account of the process of literary creation which might be matched by many others – such as the theory of 'organic form' developed by Coleridge. The theory of organic form stresses the same spontaneity and gradual weaving of structure. The model in mind is the growth of a plant or other organism until it achieves its full development and finished aesthetic shape which is held to be morally, spiritually or otherwise efficacious because of its naturalness. This is one important strand of ideas in the theoretical background of traditional Anglo-American criticism. In Barthes's passage the metaphors are altered: but not that much. There is no mention of organic growth, but magnetism is an equally natural force, and Barthes has a taste for oxymorons ('finite and perpetual', for example), like F.R. Leavis who, for instance, praised Wordsworth's 'achieved naturalness' in *Revaluation*. My point is not that Barthes and Leavis are covertly similar as critics. They are not. But they do share an equal investment – though it is unequally stressed – in the notion of spontaneous formal organisation, and in Barthes this spontaneity is sometimes ill-matched with a dominant emphasis on fragmentation. The contradiction grows directly from an overvalorisation of fragmentation and avant-garde 'Textuality' which emerges from a negative reaction to the dominant culture. But Barthes could not have articulated the theory of the dispersed self without a command of the largely unspoken continuity of subjectivity which is assumed – 'woven' – in this passage 'spontaneously'. How he worked back from this contradiction in his two remaining books will be the subject of the next two sections.

A festival of meaning

We began Chapter 4 looking at Angela Carter's Melanie looking at herself in the mirror in *The Magic Toyshop*. Here Carter deploys a widely used idea in contemporary literature and theory. The best-known version is that of the psychoanalyst Jacques Lacan in his essay 'The mirror stage' first published in its full form in 1949. The argument is that the human infant, vexed by motor inco-ordination, starts to imagine its own ideal development by seeing itself in a mirror. She or he posits an imaginary self in an ideal form. This, argues Lacan, is how the ego is formed, and, as he rather ponderously puts it: 'this form situates the agency of the ego, before its social determination, in a fictional direction.'[8] In other words, from the outset we invest heavily in an imaginary, narcissistic selfhood which is reinforced by subsequent cultural images adhering to the ideal mirror-image. Our imaginations, in a sense, imprison us in a structure which we defend and through which we try to control the environment. Before her mirror in *The Magic Toyshop*, Melanie is imaginatively exploring various images of her own sexual development in ways which cast her as a heroine. In *Roland Barthes*, Barthes's 'montage' technique tries to break the imaginary coherence which an autobiographer may wish to project as a version of his ideal ego.

Like much psychoanalytic writing, Lacan's 'The mirror stage' is best read as a fable of development rather than a strict psychogenetic account, but it is one of great resource, and strongly influenced Barthes's thinking in his later work. As always with Barthes, it is easy to interpret influence too narrowly. In an interview in 1977 he was pragmatic. Psychoanalysis was useful because he needed a psychology, and it was the only one sufficiently sensitive to selfhood as a *dramatic* structure and which offered at least some account of human love, his new topic of interest. But, he cautioned, his feelings about it were 'quite ambiguous' (*Grain*, 287–8), and in a subsequent interview he found psychoanalysis's negativity about love a problem. It is largely 'considered to be an illness from which the lover must recover, and no enriching aspects are attributed to it' (*Grain*, 292). *A Lover's Discourse* continues this theme. Barthes remarks that the lover is 'completely forsaken by the surrounding languages: ignored, disparaged or derided by them'. The lover's discourse, therefore, 'is today *of an extreme solitude*' (*LD*, 1). This is one reason why he wants the book to be read as if it is spoken *dramatically* in the first person. Like *Roland Barthes*, *A Lover's Discourse* is a book of the self spoken in character, and it too explores the 'mirror-image', the Imaginary (in Lacan's parlance), of the greedy ego.

Because the lover is now a solitary, derided being, Barthes argues, *A Lover's Discourse* is a book of retrieval. Like Foucault or Laing in their work on madness, Barthes attempts to retrieve the lover's discourse for a culture deaf to the subject, and insists – traditionally enough – that the lover and the mad person are, in some respects, alike. *A Lover's Discourse* therefore uses psychoanalysis from the perspective of the person being analysed. In short, it is an account of Lacan's idea of the Imaginary as drama, which is appropriate because 'being-in-love', for Barthes, is a kind of theatre with defined roles and expectations.

Barthes adds another thread to the argument by formulating the Freudian conception of the unconscious and conscious minds as a kind of stage on which consciousness is the proscenium and the drama itself plays out the forces of the unconscious (*LD*, 94). For Barthes, memory is a staged event in a double sense: it is staged in consciousness by unconscious impulses, and it is directed by the demands of an ego keen to promote a positive self-image (*LD*, 217). Once again, the mental topography and dynamics are formidably complex, and Barthes finds an appropriate form in the fragment which presents the self as a montage and displays the machinery of the Imaginary. *A Lover's Discourse* is made up of eighty separate 'figures'. Each gives an account of one possible mode of the lover's behaviour, and the book is alphabetically arranged to resist the creation of a distorting narrative. For Barthes, there is no 'love story' as such, except the ones which are produced by retrospective – and imaginary – rationalisation. His fragments provide a 'reservoir or thesaurus' of the lover's being. As an account 'from inside' it is stripped of outcomes or meanings. It is 'an encylopaedia of affective culture' (*LD*, 6–7) from which the Imaginary creates a theatre for the self.

In some senses *A Lover's Discourse* is kin to Barthes's structuralist projects of the 1950s and 1960s. Like them it posits a formal underlying structuring mechanism (the lover's imaginary discourse) and a more or less random set of 'figures' which can fulfil the functions set by the structuring 'language'. Here, however, the perspective is different. Whereas the earlier exercises concentrated on the formal mechanism and a negative evaluation, this later work is more concerned with the lover's imaginative investments in his figurative routines. (Perhaps regrettably, Barthes refers to the lover as 'he' throughout.) Indeed, the lover is pictured as the archetype of the meaning-maker himself: 'he is in love: he creates meaning, always and everywhere, out of nothing' (*LD*, 67). The lover's discourse is therefore 'a festival not of the senses but of meaning' (*LD*, 67–8). The similarity with the earlier work, therefore, is in another sense more with *Michelet* or *Mythologies*, in which Barthes relishes the playful imaginative energy in ideological history and modern myths respectively. The same fascinated, positive evaluation emerges in *A Lover's Discourse*. It marks a sharp change in direction in Barthes's late work. The focus now is on meaning's abundance, not its dispersal; on the human significance of the event, not the loss of selfhood.

By the standards of *Roland Barthes* and heavy 'Textuality', the lover's discourse should be censured. Lovers exist in the Imaginary, and cannot let themselves fall into dialectical bliss. They wish to create rigid imaginary worlds which coerce the loved object into static satisfactions (*LD*, 56). Lovers, Barthes comments, try to 'kidnap' loved ones to hold them in the Imaginary (*LD*, 221). Loving is therefore, by Barthes's previous standards, an unethical activity, and is described in what is customarily a negative image. The lover 'glues' himself to the Imaginary and the loved object. If Barthes's usual positive image is that of 'free play', the lover's world is one of adhesives and gummy coalescence (*LD*, 11, 51, 55, 96, 112, 128). The lover 'offers nothing in the play of the signifier' (*LD*, 96). His discourse is monological, not plural (*LD*, 204). What catches Barthes's sympathy, however, is the lover's forlorn effort to realise his impossible ambition – to live up to the factitious standards set by his own Imaginary. The lover is portrayed as driven by unconscious forces behind him, and enslaved by imagin-

ary images before him. As such he represents for Barthes a predicament increasingly conceived in classic humanist terms.

The lover is in an awful double-bind. He can gain his freedom
only by losing his loved one, and recover authentic value only
through the Zen-like '*non-will-to-possess*' which will sacrifice the
imaginary ego (*LD*, 232). Furthermore, the '*non-will-to-possess*'
cannot itself be possessed, and the lover can 'choose' his best self
only by exhaustion: 'I must manage (by the determination of what
obscure exhaustion?) to let myself drop somewhere outside language, into the inert' (*LD*, 233). But for Barthes, to drop outside
language is impossible, because language represents the permanent
state of being human and, at its best, the positive image for all
desirable change.

It would seem, therefore (and this theme will be explored further in the next section), that Barthes's ethical desideratum of
dropping into inertia is coterminous with death, and *A Lover's
Discourse* might be renamed 'A Lover's Tragedy'. Barthes elabo-
rates a half-explicit image for this (it is a version of one used before
in *S/Z*) of a room without entrance or exit. In *S/Z* this was a
positive image for the 'Text'. In *A Lover's Discourse*, however, it is
one of exclusion and entrapment (*LD*, 142, 211, 218). Thus a book
which ostensibly affirms the language of love is haunted by pain
and ambiguity. The lover is a poor, derided, self-tormented –
fortunately weak – tyrant. If Barthes finds sympathy for and pleasure in the lover's routines, it is as a classic humanist predicament.
Barthes thus turns away from the frontiers of loss, the zero degree
and the 'Text'. In ethical and psychological terms the '*non-will-to-
possess*' is his late version of these earlier values.

Barthes's portrait of the lover is of a series of contradictions.
The lover is both the idealist and the nihilist, the solitary and the
man in thrall to another. He rocks between a dream of plenitude
and a vision of annihilation. Despite the random organisation,
these polarities pulse through the book. The lover hopes for the
best and experiences the worst. He ends in misery, but he goes
lightly towards the next affair. Above all he repeats the structures
established in childhood, the painful oscillation between the bliss
of the mother-bond and the pain of her going. In another image
which usually carries negative associations, the lover's world is the
liquid world of infancy. The lover's body enjoys 'liquid expansion'
and rediscovers 'the infant body' (*LD*, 180). He re-enjoys the

range of infantile pleasurable pains: demand for total possession, fits of childish panic, craving for 'the voluptuous infantilism of sleepiness' and the 'diffuse sensuality of the incestuous embrace' (*LD*, 104). The lover wants both the genitality of maturity and the maternalism of childhood: 'the adult is superimposed upon the child. I am then two subjects in one: I want maternity *and* genitality' (*LD*, 104–5). Thus he swings from annihilation (fantasies of suicide, the ego's Imaginary in tatters) to the dream of plenitude, a fulfilled Imaginary, a paradisiacal excess beyond language (*LD*, 55). 'I love you', says Barthes, is not generous: 'It affirms itself as a force – against . . . the thousand forces of the world, which are, all of them, disparaging forces (science, *doxa*, reason, etc.)' (*LD*, 153). The lover seeks in the love object for a mirror to confirm his rapt self-image through the will to power, possession and 'happiness' (*LD*, 55, 69, 104–5, 121).

The lover is inevitably wounded, and his wound defines his subjectivity. The lover seeks to close the 'radical chasm (at the "roots" of being), which cannot be closed, and out of which the subject drains, constituting himself as a subject in the very draining' (*LD*, 189). The scenario is classically psychoanalytic: the inevitability of loss in Lacan, of discontent in Freud. The mechanisms which try to recoup these losses through the imagination are compelled to repeat them through the forces of the unconscious. But Barthes does not merely reiterate this gloomy theory, and his tone works hard to sustain the ambiguity of energetic investment in a hopeless structure. He accepts the logic of the post-Freudian position associated with Lacan and Derrida, but works against its logic. Lacan and Derrida argue that the psychological and intellectual worlds are radically decentred. There is no fundamental ground for human existence or understanding. Culture, thought and behaviour are therefore efforts to construct an imaginary presence to cover this absence. In *Roland Barthes* and his writing on 'Textuality', Barthes dramatises this argument as the self-dismantling game of literary writing itself. But *A Lover's Discourse* carefully reverses the terms and makes a positive investment in illusion, tenderness, sympathy, and so on which are 'a miraculous crystallization of presence' (presence is a key, negative term in Derrida) (*LD*, 224–5). Barthes accepts the argument about the basis of absence, and so on, but, as here, he constructs from it an ethical virtue: in mutual kindness 'we mother each other' (*LD*,

224). From loss come the voluntary transactions of mutual need. In other words, from absence (the mother has gone) we create a presence which has an efficacy coefficient with its originating negative.

As we shall see, this impressive argument is continued in Barthes's next book, *Camera Lucida*, but it gains its power in *A Lover's Discourse* from being embedded in a form which seems to put the case for the fragmented world of deconstruction. The book of lovers pleads for the rescue of a social group of whom modern culture has lost sight, and dramatises a solitary discourse presented unequivocally as manipulative and illusory. But the first-person pronoun used throughout has a double effect. The 'I' of the lover's discourse is, technically, a linguistic 'shifter'. The theory of the 'shifter', developed by Barthes's friend Émile Benveniste, influenced him deeply. The argument is that personal pronouns are rare examples of 'empty' signs whose very function is to create an open signifier.[9] For instance, we all use 'I', but used by Rick Rylance it indicates something different from when it is used by another. In *Roland Barthes*, Barthes develops the utopian implication: 'Can we even imagine the freedom and, so to speak, the erotic fluidity of a collectivity which would speak only in pronouns and shifters, each person never saying anything . . . legal whatsoever, and in which the *vagueness of difference* . . . would be language's most precious value?' (*RB*, 166). He imagines a utopia in which the boundaries between the self and another are endlessly porous; in which difference is abolished because we can, as it were, inhabit each other's language world. This is essentially what the 'I' of *A Lover's Discourse* enacts. We think 'he is the lover', but read 'I am the lover'. The 'vagueness of difference' performs a powerful ethical transaction.

This is why many of the most powerful images in Barthes's late work involve the idea of *circulation* rather than the violent conceptions of loss figured in the 'Text'. The idea of circulation is crucial because it refuses hierarchy or essential value, but Barthes's image is carefully ambiguous. It is associated with the circulation of intellectual property (of which the intertext is the utopian version) and of commodities and capital (*LD*, 70).[10] But circulation is also an ideal economy with infinite 'open expenditure' (*LD*, 85). It is associated with non-possessive sexuality ('cruising') and a relaxation of the Imaginary: 'let desire circulate within me' (*LD*, 232).

The ethical exchange of *A Lover's Discourse* is therefore the circulation, and eventual braiding, of monologues: 'It is as if the proto-actor, the madman, and the lover refused to posit themselves as the hero of speech and to submit to adult language, the social language to which they are prompted by . . . the language of universal neurosis' (*LD*, 205). By not being heroic, the 'shifters' of the lover's discourse are open. In content, the book presents a part of the culture's repressed as a monologue. In form, it imbricates the reader by shifting his or her subjectivity into dialogue.

Barthes's descriptions of the lover's Imaginary return to earlier themes. The lover's images function like the circulation of capital, and he becomes an alienated worker in his own imaginative factory: 'I have nothing to decide; the amorous (imaginary) machinery here operates all by itself within me; like a workman of the electronic age, or like the dunce in the last row of the classroom, all I have to do is *be there*' (*LD*, 64). The Imaginary is a machine running by itself (*LD*, 160, 220). Barthes connects this to a familiar argument (found also in *The Fashion System*) that 'Mass Culture is a machine for showing desire: here is what must interest you, it says, as if it guessed that men were incapable of finding what to desire by themselves' (*LD*, 136–7). But this is the only point at which these older arguments surface, and they are more complex than those made earlier by Marcuse, Deleuze and Guattari – from whom the idea of the 'desiring machine' is taken – or the Situationist Guy Debord in *Society of the Spectacle*, (1967). These writers argued that mass-cultural products distort an aboriginal authentic desire by addictive force-feeding. Barthes's argument is both more complex and more pessimistic, and is again derived from Lacan. The lover's desire is always substitutional because it compensates for necessary infantile loss. But it is also, as in this passage on mass culture, baffled. We are incapable of discovering our desires because they are constructed through the complex circuitry of Imaginary and social evaluations: we discover the desirability of our love object through the desire of others for that object (*LD*, 136–7). We want because others want, even in our most intimate relationships.

Often Barthes expresses the power of the Imaginary by its physicality. The lover is 'immobilised, nose stuck to the image (the mirror)' (*LD*, 189), and Barthes posits an 'inward body' which can be suddenly awakened by a word, thought or image. The effect is often traumatic – like music gone wrong ('a din') or a flood, 'everything is (more or less rapidly) ravaged'. The 'imaginary body' is 'so "coherent" (coalescent) that I can experience it only in the form of a generalised pang', like a blush, a sudden panic, or a glimpse 'of my own destruction' (*LD*, 200–1). Barthes's idea of the body is one of the most complex areas of his work, and sometimes he is aligned with protests against the separation of mind and body in much Western, Christian discourse. This argument is familiar and the suppression or malformation of sexual instincts by an overemphasis on the mind, will or spirit is often stressed. But it has other dimensions too.

R.D. Laing suggested in *The Divided Self* that schizoid individuals display an antipathy towards, or reification of, their bodies. Instead of the body constituting the core of the 'true self' it 'is felt more as one object among other objects in the world than as the core of the individual's own being' (*Laing*, 71). As a result the personality is a collage of incoherent 'fragments'. In Laing the body 'grounds' the self's ontological security. This claim is common, and is made by poststructuralists like Foucault and, especially, feminists such as Kristeva and Cixous – though they stress its multivalence and diversity. In these theories the body is not a stable entity but a site of rhythms, pulses and energy, and of diverse practices and transgressive pleasures. It is easy to see the relevance of this to the feminist opposition to patriarchy which, like culture in general in some versions of the argument, is seen to regiment aboriginal diversity and energy.

Sometimes Barthes's concept of the body is also described as an ethico-political entity, valuable because its energetic plurality disturbs ruling opinion.[11] But this is opposed by Jonathan Culler, who objects to what he sees as its mystification and idealisation of nature over culture.[12] On the face of it, Culler's argument has some plausibility. After all, many critics who propose the radical argument about 'the body' would object to F.R. Leavis's idea that one can feel 'life' in excellent literary works. But Barthes's ideas are more complex, partly because they are inconsistent and not a little contradictory. Barthes himself acknowledged this in *Roland Barthes*. The idea of the body, he remarks, functions for him as what he calls a 'fashion word', by which he means a habit of deploying certain terms without thinking them through properly (*RB*, 127). Later he talks about 'body' as a 'mana-word . . . a word

whose ardent, complex, ineffable, and somehow sacred signification gives the illusion that by this word one might answer for
everything' (*RB*, 129). So Barthes is conscious of the way the
natural body can provide 'the illusion' of a grounded discourse.

Barthes's confession reflects aspects of his practice. Sometimes
he writes as though the body were a term of last appeal, or an
existential or ethical guarantor. Morality, he writes, is 'the thinking of the body in a state of language'. It is 'the precise opposite of
ethics' (*RB*, 145). One of the problems with this kind of statement
is that I am not sure what 'thinking of the body in a state of
language' means, or why it constitutes the difference between
morality and ethics. It seems to imply only that morality is instinctive. At other times the same idea is offered with an ironic
inflection, as when Barthes describes his selection of beliefs by
their bodily 'fit', as though he were trying on clothes (*RB*, 156–7).
At yet other times the body seems exempt from the objections
Barthes makes against other concepts like the *doxa* or myth. Repetition, for instance, is fine in the body, but becomes a wearying
stereotype elsewhere (*RB*, 71, 112). Indeed, the body is sometimes
asserted to be the very opposite of the stereotype, which is 'that
emplacement of discourse *where the body is missing*, where one is
sure the body is not' (*RB*, 90). Here the argument again relies on
instinct ('where one is sure'), and on using the body as a token for
authenticity (bad discourse *lacks* the body). The body is the irre-
ducibly individual, unique, authentic, existentially irreplaceable:
'*my body is not the same as yours*' (*RB*, 117). It distinguishes him
from even his closest allies in the *Tel Quel* group (*RB*, 31–2).

One can understand why Barthes is driven towards this kind of
position. If it is argued that the self is constituted in language, and
language is a matter of culture, and culture, according to Barthes
and Freud, is based on suppression, then the idea of the non-
intellectual body can attractively defend the integrity of the individual self. In one section of *Roland Barthes* entitled 'My Head Is
Confused', Barthes repairs his intellectual confusion by writing:
'And yet: *at the level of his body*, his head never gets confused' (*RB*,
176). These kinds of arguments are familiar from conventional
wisdom (follow your heart, not your head) and from intellectual
and literary debate. They are, for instance, a cornerstone of the
thinking of D.H. Lawrence, a writer who has more in common
with Barthes than might be supposed. Both Lawrence and Barthes

were, for instance, anti-collectivist thinkers driven increasingly towards an individualism which writes off the collective as inevitably malign.[13] Both attacked ideas of the 'social personality' and, especially, the will; and both used innovative language and formal organisation to break down conventional conceptions of the self in writing. Both also developed positive theories of the bodily and the sexual as radical oppositions to the conventional, the mental, the ideological and the social. Though Barthes attacked the belief that 'sexual liberation' was itself a panacea (*RB*, 65–6), he was reacting against the inflation of this idea in the 1960s, and both he and Lawrence believed that sex is essentially non-social (*RB*, 165).

So the discursive function of the body in Barthes is in some respects like that of sexuality in Lawrence. Both represent an opposition to the prevailing culture, though Barthes's ideas in this respect are much more ironically conceived than those of Lawrence. In Barthes's work, there is an alternation between this view and an equally steady wish to unsettle its privileged status. We have seen this already in his remarks on 'mana' or 'fashion' words, but he also diminishes the idea elsewhere. Barthes's discourse, like Brecht's, is essentially anti-heroic. The hero is defined in *A Lover's Discourse* as 'The one who has the last word' (*LD*, 209), and Barthes fights against the idea that any term should have the last word. Thus the body is consistently mocked in, for instance, the illustration which closes *Roland Barthes* and is used on the cover of the English translation. Taken from Diderot's *Encyclopédie*, it is an ugly, veinous figure titled 'Anatomie'; it is captioned 'To write the body', and described as an 'awkward, fibrous, shaggy, raveled thing, a clown's coat'. In *A Lover's Discourse* the body is a conduit for the infantile unconscious, and for the greedy Imaginary which slurps the messages it wants to hear from the loved one's presence. The idea of the body as having a sovereign integrity is, firmly, an illusion.

In Barthes, then, the body has an unstable, fluctuating status which makes it difficult to deliver a pure message, though myths of the body, as Michael Moriarty notes, remained an abiding preoccupation for him from *Michelet* on.[14] At the opening of *A Lover's Discourse* Barthes writes that the lover is '*marked*, like the trace of a code' (*LD*, 4: translation adapted). He means that his actions are structured by the repertoire of approved behaviours for lovers, and 'in other times this would have been the code of courtly love, or the Carte du Tendre'. But Barthes's image is interesting because it suggests a more deep-lying determination of behaviour, like the way software codes a computer, or genetic codes 'programme' the body.[15] So it would seem here that what biotechnologists call the 'warmware' has no more existential authority than any other component of the organic machine. The Imaginary is therefore imperishable, and if an authentic physicality does exist, it is only ever glimpsed fugitively, for the human subject's nose remains pressed close to the mirror of its own ego. Angela Carter seems to follow this argument, too, in *The Magic Toyshop*. The novel begins:

> The summer she was fifteen, Melanie discovered she was made of flesh and blood. O, my America, my new found land. She embarked on a tranced voyage, exploring the whole of herself, clambering her own mountain ranges, penetrating the moist richness of her secret valleys, a physiological Cortez, da Gama or Mungo Park. For hours she stared at herself, naked, in the mirror of her wardrobe . . . [16]

Here, as we noted above, begins her adolescent mirror stage. By the end of the novel Melanie has grown from adolescence to maturity, has confronted violent patriarchy and, defeating it, is poised to begin a fuller life. The ending, therefore, as Carter commented in an interview, reverses *Paradise Lost*: the humans evict the tyrannical God and take possession of the garden.[17] The novel closes with the lover's 'wild surmise' at abundant possibilities. 'Wild surmise' is a quotation from Keats's sonnet 'On First Looking into Chapman's Homer', in which the exhilarating literary experience of discovering Chapman's translation of Homer is compared to Cortez's 'discovery' of the Pacific. The ending, therefore, connects to the beginning, when exactly the same metaphor is used for Melanie's discovery of her sexuality. The novel turns in a circle; it is not a progress from narcissism, naivety and cultural conditioning at the beginning to maturity, freedom and existential authenticity at the close. Though things have been discovered and learnt, Melanie is caught just as deeply in the literary and the Imaginary at the end as she is at the beginning. The Imaginary is as omnipresent as it is in Barthes. Value is not a matter of reaching 'truth', 'the body', the Pacific, or any other 'last word'. It is, as ever in Barthes, a mode of play within the conditioning terms of a discourse and situation.

Throughout his career, however, Barthes devised utopias. His justification for this was the usual one: utopias release thought from the difficulties of the everyday, and generate perspective and possibility. Barthes compares reality and utopia to two sides of a coin: they are the same thing, but each presents a different facet (*RB*, 76). Barthes's best-known utopia is *Empire of Signs* (1970), written at the height of his enthusiasm for the 'Text' and – he claims in *Roland Barthes* – his only successful book (*RB*, 156). *Empire of Signs* is a book about Japan, but it is an ideal Japan – presented beautifully in the French edition, with colour photographs, but rather dingily in the English version, which somewhat spoils the point. Barthes's Japan is knowingly unreal, though he equivocally argued that the book was both 'my Japan, a system of signs I call Japan', and a kind of historical reality:

> Japan is in the very special position of a feudal society that transformed itself in less than a century, through extraordinary economic expansionism. The ethical presence of feudalism maintains in this intensely 'technicized' – and not really Americanized – society a set of values, an art of living, which is probably rather fragile in the light of history, and which must be linked to the fundamental absence of monotheism. (*Grain*, 83–4)

This earnest dissertation on social and economic history introduces covert values: 'not really Americanized', 'an art of living', and so on. Japan in *Empire of Signs* represents for Barthes a desirable alternative to the West. Tokyo, he says, is an image of the Lacanian subject (*RB*, 99), a 'precious paradox: it does possess a centre, but this centre is empty' (*Empire*, 30). Like the non-hierarchical forms of Japanese meals, or style of interior decoration, or art of packaging (which puts as much emphasis on the beautiful layers as on the gift), Japan represents the desirable opposite of the Western craving for the core, the event, the fact or truth. Barthes's Japan is full of these Zen-like parables and examples. It is the geography and culture of the 'Text' itself (*Empire*, 55), emphasising the disadvantages of Western rationalism. At best, it is a modern version of the 'fantastic voyage' of which *Gulliver's Travels* is the best-known example in English.

But the argument is problematic. Though Barthes strives to construct what he calls a 'counter-mythology', a 'happiness of signs' (*Grain*, 158), *Empire of Signs* in fact falls prey to mythology too, largely because it is easily read as another Western indulgence in chinoiserie, what Edward Said has called 'Orientalism' – that is, the projection by the West on to the East of qualities which have more to do with Western hopes and needs than with Eastern realities.[18] *Empire of Signs* in fact creates the thrill of the cruising tourist (the book reads almost like an erotic quest by Robbe-Grillet) and the kind of enclosed utopia which Barthes perversely finds in the Marquis de Sade (*SFL*, 17). As such it is somewhat different from, for example, the contemporaneous accounts of Japanese sexuality by Angela Carter in her essays for *New Society* (collected in *Nothing Sacred*) or her stories in *Fireworks* (1974). *Empire of Signs* can also be seen as an elided version of the Maoist enthusiasm for China which a number of French intellectuals, including Foucault and the *Tel Quel* group, were projecting in this period, and with which Barthes occasionally fellow-travelled. Either way, his enthusiasm for Japan has an uneasy relation to that very authoritarianism – be it Maoist or feudal – which his ethics and politics reject. The next section, therefore, will look at the re-encounter not with the Imaginary, but with the real.

The self surprised

This section is concerned with Barthes's last and in some ways most challenging book, *Camera Lucida* (1980). Nominally about photography, *Camera Lucida* is a moving enquiry into human loss, written after the death of his mother, with whom he lived through most of his adult life. As a book about loss *Camera Lucida* revisits themes which haunt his career and had been momentarily celebrated in the ecstatic losses of the 'Text' in the late 1960s. What is different is that these privations return not as jubilant release, but void. *Camera Lucida*, therefore, continues the revision of the poststructuralist positions for which Barthes had become famous in the English-speaking world. It puts a classically humanist case for representational realism, for the fructifying virtues of memory, and the claims of other beings in the psychology of postmodern individualism. It is Barthes's most heart-searchingly frank, least gamesome, book, whose distinctive note is sounded early. 'Who could help me?' Barthes asks on the second page (*CL*, 4). He is speaking of his reflections on photography, but the plea involves the reader in a directness of appeal which is unique in Barthes. 'Who could help me?' is as much about mourning as about photography. But the pain – so persistent that many believe Barthes lost his will to live – is formulated with a moving generosity which makes *Camera Lucida* a most powerful elegy. Alongside *Mythologies*, it is probably Barthes's most accessible work, and its formality creates a poignancy and dignity which somewhat resemble, in English prose, William Godwin's beautiful *Memoirs of the Author of a Vindication of the Rights of Woman* (1798) about his wife Mary Wollstonecraft.

Barthes's new arguments developed gradually, and involved a shift from the largely ideological and 'Textual' thinking of the earlier work to what he calls in *Camera Lucida*, 'an "ontological" desire' which 'overcomes' him (*CL*, 3). This book, then, enquires into what constitutes the self most essentially; it is likened by Annette Lavers to a 'hermeneutic thriller' and by Michael Moriarty to a quest or adventure.[19] Indeed, many critics comment that the narrative and relaxed discursive manner of *Camera Lucida* is similar to that of the novel Barthes acknowledged that he wished to write. It is certainly very different from the fragmented methods and prickly style of earlier work. In part this is consequent on a change in his conception of language. Hitherto his ideas about language had been compatible with Saussure's idea of *langue*, an overarching system which Barthes, in his structuralist phase, thought malign or, in his 'Textual' phase, liberatingly impersonal. In his last three books, however, Barthes moves towards a much more transactional view. Language is now conceived as a human instrument with intersubjective dimensions.

The transition between these views was not smooth. In *Roland Barthes* he argues initially that connotation, not the message, is the true subject of linguistics (*RB*, 79). This is conventional enough for Barthes. It is the linguistics of the 'Text', the ebb and flow of plural signification, and it rejects what he calls the 'pseudo-linguistics' of structuralism (*RB*, 124). Barthes, therefore, abandons scientificity, but retains an objectivist conception of language. Later, however, he takes a different line, arguing that a 'linguistics of value' must work in a more intersubjective register: '*notification* (I plant my message and assign my auditor) and *signature* (I display myself, I cannot avoid displaying myself)' (*RB*, 166). This interest in interpersonal dynamics is mirrored, as we have seen, in the importance placed on pronominal 'shifters', and *A Lover's Discourse* pushes the argument further. He retains some of the scientistic vocabulary of the earlier work, but lightens it towards mere metaphor. He repeats his old theme – 'official linguistics concerns itself only with the message' (*LD*, 183) – but now recommends the study of 'two necessary linguistic series: that of interlocution (speaking to another) and delocution (speaking about someone)' (*LD*, 184). This is the emotional 'reverberation' which converts the lover into a 'monstrous receiver' and the message itself into an oxymoronic 'intelligible din'. By this stage, therefore, the grip of the linguistics of *langue* has relaxed completely, and Barthes's interest is centred entirely on the contortions of intersubjective communication which he calls 'the ear which speaks' (*LD*, 202).

At the same time, he also registers dissatisfaction with the idea that impersonal language should be the arbiter of value, as in his 'Textual' phase. The lover's discourse, he comments, is non-'Textual', with little significatory play. But Barthes has a rather unsteady sense of the consequences. Sometimes he sustains the 'Text' as an ideal value; at other times the lover is defended from judgements (including 'Textual' ones) which lie outside his subjective discourse. For example, in *Roland Barthes* he is very severe on domestic 'scenes'. They are stereotypes, genre paintings, degradingly ritualised bouts of violence, a 'cancer of language' compared to the free play of 'Text' (*RB*, 159–60). But in *A Lover's Discourse* Barthes is much more sympathetic. He now understands the 'scene' as a piece of theatre, a psychologically necessary, ritualised 'exchange of language goods', a pair of matching soliloquies which are not merely stereotypical (*LD*, 204–5). He has developed here a new sense of the human dynamics of events, and what was earlier seen as cancerous outpouring has been rethought as a gamesome way of containing or sublimating violence in which lovers 'joust' before falling exhausted. The stereotype continues to provide their script, but the significance of the event does not lie only there.

A Lover's Discourse collapses other key Barthesian terms. Bliss can be childish, not (as in *S/Z*) mature; and 'writing' (a key poststructuralist term derived from Derrida) is characterised as violent, alien and wilful. This is quite at odds with the kind of ethical efficacy in a beneficial loss of hierarchy envisioned for the 'Text'. In the section 'The Dedication', Barthes makes the point that writers personalise their work by dedicating it to a loved one, 'like a cake or an embroidered slipper', but it has an independent purposiveness:

> Writing is dry, obtuse; a kind of steamroller, writing advances, indifferent, indelicate, and would kill 'father, mother, lover' rather than deviate from its fatality (enigmatic though that fatality may be). When I write, I must acknowledge this fact (which, according to my Image-repertoire, lacerates me): there is no benevolence within writing, rather a terror: it smothers the other, who, far from perceiving the gift in it, reads there instead an assertion of mastery, of power, of pleasure, of solitude. Whence the cruel paradox of the dedication: I seek at all costs to give you what smothers you. (*LD*, 78–9)

As always, this is spoken in the character of the lover, but two things are evident. First, writing is now negatively characterised and associated with death, murder, terrorism, amoral purpose and the will to power. Second, the context is now understood to be *intersubjective*. Writing no longer stands aloof, waiting to grant the bliss of the 'Textual' devotee. Barthes does not reject writing (which would be as pointless as arguing with a steamroller), but he does complicate its ethical status. The 'Text' does not produce, always and everywhere, an undeniable good, and Barthes shifts the focus from 'Text' to context.

In *Camera Lucida* Barthes develops the argument in two ways. Most obviously, the subject of the book is photography, not writing, but he also shifts the discussion from formal structures (or polemically informal structures like 'Text') to questions of personal identity. Photography is fundamentally different from writing, he argues, for two reasons. First, language is endless, but a photograph is finite. By this he means that an image cannot be transformed in time. A moving photograph of his mother, for example, retains its power in a way writing cannot because writing translates emotion as it moves forward. It is often said, for instance, that writing about personal distress helps to resolve it and the function of tragedy or elegy is to 'cope' with death. The fact that photographs are produced mechanically, Barthes argues, preserves their emotional power from the interference of textual catharsis: 'The Photograph is violent: not because it shows violent things, but because on each occasion *it fills the sight by force*, and because in it nothing can be refused or transformed' (*CL*, 91). The subjective transaction is categorically different to that experienced in writing.

The second difference arises because photographs have an authenticity which writing cannot match. 'It is the misfortune (but perhaps the voluptuous pleasure) of language not to be able to authenticate itself,' he writes (*CL*, 85). This is the anti-representationalist position we encountered earlier. It claims that because language cannot adequately represent extra-linguistic reality, it is inevitably epistemologically unreliable. Language, writes Barthes in *Camera Lucida*, 'is, by nature, fictional', whereas photography 'does not invent; it is authentication itself; the (rare) artifices it permits are not probative; they are, on the contrary, trick pictures: the photograph is laborious only when it fakes'. Photography 'can lie as to the meaning of a thing . . . never as to its existence' (*CL*, 87). Barthes derives the emotional power of photography from the fact that, unlike writing, it offers up the real: 'Every photograph is a certificate of presence' (*CL*, 87); and 'from the phenomenological viewpoint, in the Photograph, the power of authentication exceeds the power of representation' (*CL*, 89).

These are dubious arguments, and Barthes seems wilfully naive about photographic fakery, but to examine them at the theoretical level alone is to mistake their point. Though Barthes maintains that he is looking for aesthetic universals (actually a very un-Barthesian project), the real subject of *Camera Lucida* is the particular psychology of the self intersecting with the public domain. This complex issue takes general and particular forms. First, in personal terms, *Camera Lucida* asks how one can locate an authentic core to one's self when both language and the self itself – in Lacan's theory of the Imaginary – are disposed towards fiction. Second, if this is obtainable, how can the intimate self be articulated in a world of mass stereotype where individuals are reduced to formula versions of themselves (the British tabloid press does this relentlessly)? Third, if one can found a theory of realism on the basis of the way art objects move us emotionally, how does Barthes accommodate this to his habitual anti-realism?

These complicated issues are best taken separately, beginning with Barthes's conception of selfhood in *Camera Lucida*. His interest in photography centres on its emotional impact. If fake photographs exist, he says, they quickly become 'laborious': one can distinguish the fake from the real by an instinctive quality of emotional response: fakes bore. Real photographs, on the other hand, are emotionally affecting. This is the latest example of a tendency we have noticed before – Barthes's accreditation of the 'amateur', spontaneous instinct. This lightly worn irrationalism curls in and out of his later work in dialogue with other arguments, but *Camera Lucida* puts it at the centre of attention. Barthes is not interested in structure or in form, but in emotional authenticity. He therefore distinguishes between two kinds of response to photography: those in which he invests his '*studium*' and those in which he invests his '*punctum*'. The former is a 'general enthusiasm' (*CL*, 26), 'of the order of *liking*, not of *loving*'. There is nothing to distinguish it from other enthusiasms for books, clothes or entertainment (*CL*, 27). The *punctum*, however, is a piercing moment of delight or pain, a surprise of the self, a mystery (*CL*, 27, 28, 51).

The difference between *studium* and *punctum* is similar to other binary distinctions, especially that between 'work' and 'Text'. Indeed, the *punctum* is sometimes described in ways reminiscent of 'Textuality'. It is the experience of lapse, break or mutation from everyday life (*CL*, 49). It is conveyed by oxymorons: a 'floating flash', sharp and vague, a silent cry (*CL*, 53). It is kin to infantile experiences, madness, religious mysticism or the primitive. However, there is a major difference between the *punctum* and the experience of 'Text'. Barthes writes that some photographs provoke 'tiny jubilations, as if they referred to a stilled centre, an erotic or lacerated value buried in myself' (*CL*, 16). In other words, what happens during *punctum* is a realisation of something *already present* in the self, however inchoate; whereas the experience of 'Text' is one of loss. 'Textuality' evaporates the self; *punctum* helps to define it (*CL*, 82). *Punctum* operates on an individuality unconscious of depths which are discovered in the sudden surprises of deep feeling. *Camera Lucida* therefore tries to 'extend this individuality to a science of the subject whose name is of little importance to me provided it attains (as has not yet occurred) to a generality which neither reduces nor crushes me' (*CL*, 18). The interest in this unreduced, uncrushed self (it is difficult not to think of Barthes's image of language as a steamroller here) is what distinguishes *Camera Lucida* from the works on 'Text'.

Camera Lucida is preoccupied by the boundary of the personal and the public. Its analyses of reproduced photographs examine public situations (news shots, portraits, street pictures) and elegantly release from them the affects Barthes personally cherishes – the fascinating, incidental detail or distracting expression. Sometimes his remarks have a political dimension, as in the photograph of 'William Casby, Born a Slave'. Sometimes they have a singular whimsy. But the point is that Barthes's response is unyieldingly personal. There is no pretence (as there sometimes is when he speaks about 'Text') that the *punctum* is objective. It is a mode of this particular self. So *Camera Lucida*, shifting between the public and the private, plays a double game. It displays a self, but also keeps it aloof, and Barthes regularly returns to the theme of privacy, which he describes as a 'political right' (*CL*, 15). The paradox of the book is that it examines the private 'zone' (his term) it wants to protect, and Barthes cleverly works the border between uttering 'interiority without yielding intimacy' (*CL*, 98).

Again, an old theme is given a new twist. In *Roland Barthes* and *A Lover's Discourse* Barthes was concerned with the theatricalisation of the self. The personality has successive layers without a centre, rather like an onion. What is different in *Camera Lucida* is that these layers cover a central self which holds the various performances together. Hence the book deploys, for the relativist Barthes, unusually humanist metaphors of 'depth', 'presence', 'religious substance', 'the beyond' or 'the absolute' (*CL*, 57, 59, 60, 82), and what is revealed by the *punctum* is rather similar to other autobiographical searchings such as Wordsworth's 'spots of time' or modernist epiphanies and 'moments of being'. In the *punctum* one glimpses, but does not comprehend, the dynamic originating presence: 'the *punctum*, then, is a kind of subtle *beyond* – as if the image launched desire beyond what it permits us to see . . . toward the absolute excellence of a being, body and soul together' (*CL*, 59). Barthes is an unspiritual writer, but he uses the language of mysticism to capture psychological modalities (his subject here is actually erotic photography). The *punctum* collects classical forms of human behaviour.

Camera Lucida hovers over paradoxes, trying to establish a more dynamic model for the interaction between subject and object. The *punctum* 'is an addition: it is what I add to the photograph and *what is nonetheless already there*.' (*CL*, 55). The technology of image-making, the mass circulation of images and the modern abundance of reflective surfaces (glass, steel and polish) alters the modern sense of the self. We literally see ourselves more, and this has an inevitable psychological impact: 'the Photograph is the advent of myself as other: a cunning dissociation of consciousness from identity' (*CL*, 12). This develops the 'mirror-stage' argument Barthes took from Lacan. The ego's sense of self is fictional, and one reinforces it by flattering images. But Barthes asks why we select these images, not others. Why does this particular image yield a *punctum*, while that one is indifferent? In addition, Barthes now conceives the Imaginary as unstable. In *A Lover's Discourse* he gives the impression that the lover's Imaginary is a coherent field, with formalised routines and outcomes. But when one is photographed, one's Imaginary consciousness is subject to severe strains in the struggle to 'imitate oneself':

> The portrait-photograph is a closed field of forces. Four image-repertoires intersect here, oppose and distort each other. In front of the lens, I am at the same time: the one I think I am, the one I want others to think I am, the one the photographer thinks I am, and the one he makes use of to exhibit his art. In other words, a strange action: I do not stop imitating myself, and because of this, each time I am (or let myself be) photographed, I invariably suffer from a sensation of inauthenticity, sometimes of imposture (comparable to certain nightmares). In terms of image-repertoire, the Photograph (the one I *intend*) represents the very subtle moment when, to tell the truth, I am neither subject nor object but a subject who feels he is becoming an object: I then experience a micro-version of death (of parenthesis): I am truly becoming a spectre. (*CL*, 13–14)

This very remarkable passage deserves close attention.

The first point is that this is a much more complex set of psychological dynamics than any offered in Barthes's earlier work. The criss-crossing of psychological forces, and the vertiginous layerings of the self, produce a much more sophisticated picture than that envisioned in encounters with 'Literature', mythology, the body, the 'Text' or the Image-repertoires of self and lover. Second, there is a modification of the Image-repertoire, or 'mirror-stage' theory. This takes two forms. First, Barthes insists that imaginary identity is vitiating. The imaginary self is an enfeebled, ghostly self, a nightmare. In a sense this is a return to his position in *Roland Barthes*, but in another way it is not. Barthes's second amendment to the Image-repertoire theory concerns the notion of imitation. This idea is complex, because several separate psychological actions coexist within it. The individual imitates the ego's sense of the self (the person I would like myself to be) *and* the social image one wants to project ('the one I want others to think I am'). But at the same time, imitation implies a consciousness separate from the act, and an awareness of 'imposture'. This assumes another 'self' beyond the routines of the various Image-repertoires. What is altered from *Roland Barthes*, therefore, is the acknowledgement of a separate self beyond fragmentation: the self which cannot in itself be described, but can fragment the Imaginary.

The vertigo induced by this line of thought is disorientating, and is one reason why the language of writers like Lacan, who think along these lines, is so difficult: how can one find a language to describe a self which cannot be described? The problem is familiar if we try to articulate our own most heartfelt selves. We find ourselves caught in endless revisions – 'No, that's not quite it' – and hesitations. For Barthes the difficulty of this description was a continual preoccupation. In interviews in the 1970s he stressed that it was the *complexity* of the subjective life which interested him, and expressed a typical dissatisfaction with neat formulae: 'I don't like the idea of a unitary subject, I prefer the play of a kaleidoscope: you give it a tap, and the little bits of coloured glass form a new pattern' (*Grain*, 204). Barthes follows this credo in his last three books. He is untroubled by the dizzying revisions, because they mirror the self itself and the intellectual difficulty of the project. What is exciting about *Camera Lucida* is its willingness to confront the uncertainties of introspection. It is a dramatisation of thinking about the self thinking about itself. It is also a contribution to the psychology of mourning, an act of self-inspection and indecision typical of a period of bereavement. Therefore, the provisional conceptualisations the book proposes (especially at the beginning, because its argument develops like a narrative) always have a supplementary dimension to be considered. As a result it is impossible to summarise Barthes's 'beliefs': his beliefs lie in their continual evolution.

For instance, what haunts Barthes's meditations on imitation cited above is the role of the unconscious. The unconscious is clearly at work in the drive to imitate, for why else should we be compelled to go through routines experienced as nightmarish? But the unconscious also figures in *Camera Lucida* in a positive sense. The *punctum* is, by definition, a reaction called forth unconsciously, spontaneously. If the Imaginary, as Barthes puts it, dissociates consciousness from identity, then the *punctum* puts the two back into connection. It heals the rift between the sensation of inauthenticity one has in being photographed and the authenticity which Barthes claims is the very mode of existence of photography itself. What the *punctum* calls forth is a self *surprised* by its own authenticity, a healthful discovery which goes past the image towards the core.

All these experiences – the sense of inauthenticity and division, the compulsion to repeat 'nightmares', the desire to reconnect with the thing which has been lost – are figures of mourning; and Barthes's relation to photography acts as a synecdoche of a more general discussion of mortality. He argues that photography is kin not to painting but to theatre. The argument is part historical (photography was initially an art of spectacle) and part a 'singular' connection ('perhaps I am the only one who sees it', *CL*, 31) made between the origins of theatre in the 'cult of the Dead' and photography as 'a kind of primitive theatre, a kind of *Tableau Vivant*, a figuration of the motionless and made-up face beneath which we see the dead' (*CL*, 32). Once again, this theoretically contentious argument is more important considered psychologically. Barthes is using theoretical discussion to find a language both to distance and to enable the expression of pain. He thinks about all those photographs whose subjects are now dead: 'I am the point of reference for every photograph, and this is what generates my astonishment in addressing myself to the fundamental question: why is it I am alive *here and now*?' (*CL*, 84). The tone of remarks like this is extraordinary: Barthes is '*astonished*' (not horrified or appalled) by the charnel house which photography summons up.

The most important photograph in *Camera Lucida* is not, in fact, reproduced. It is one of Barthes's mother as a young girl, which he finds while sorting through her effects. Its impact is a startling version of the *punctum* 'in which I discover her: a sudden awakening, outside of "likeness", a *satori* [the state of inner emptiness in Zen] in which words fail, the rare, perhaps unique evidence of the "So, yes, so much and no more"' (*CL*, 109). It splits language – 'words fail' – and reveals a purely mental conception, adequate – 'so much and no more' – to the object outside the self: 'I discover her'. Much of Part Two of *Camera Lucida* meditates on this at personal and aesthetic levels. In personal terms the 'Winter Garden Photograph' (as Barthes calls it) is the means by which identity is established; while in aesthetic terms it presents the problem of representational realism in a new light. The two levels intimately connect. The 'Winter Garden Photograph' gives him the 'air' of his mother:

> The air (I use this word, lacking anything better, for the expression of truth) is a kind of intractable supplement of identity, what is given as an act of grace, stripped of any 'importance': the air expresses the subject, in so far as that subject assigns itself no importance. In this veracious photograph, the being I love, whom I have loved, is not separated from itself: at last it coincides. And, mysteriously, this coincidence is a kind of metamorphosis. All the photographs of my mother which I was looking through were a little like so many masks; at last, suddenly the mask vanished: there remained a soul, ageless but not timeless, since this air was the person I used to know, consubstantial with her face, each day of her long life. (*CL*, 109)

Here are persisting Barthesian themes – the loss of the mask and egoistic 'importance', the oxymoronic coincidence of simultaneity and supplement, the suddenness of revelation – but new ideas emerge too. This is a 'veracious' process, the discovery of truth couched, once more, in the language of mysticism. As with Wordsworth, this moment in a particular individual history is an act of memory in which what is lost is recovered, and the recollection unites with present perception. The 'being I love . . . is not separated from itself'; and neither is the self which perceives and remembers. In the *punctum*, and most dramatically in this moment whose intimacy Barthes cannot compromise by reproducing the picture (by definition it would mean little to another: *CL*, 73), the self is shocked into authenticity.

Surprise is crucial. Barthes calls it a 'counter-memory' (*CL*, 91), after Foucault's idea that the powerful fictionalise the past for their own interests, and these versions need to be countered. In the theory of counter-memory, a more authentic memory defamiliarises the customary. This is why the *punctum* can be violent or painful; it disrupts and realigns the self's version of the past. In

The Pleasure of the Text memory is abolished, but counter-memory reintegrates the self. What the 'Winter Garden Photograph' reveals, Barthes writes, is not 'a secret thing (monster or treasure)' but the 'thread which drew me toward Photography' (*CL*, 73). Barthes alters an encounter which negates the self (the 'Text' or zero degree) to a threaded connection in which the photograph and the self are pulled reciprocally together, and authenticate one another by the very surprise they practise on the customary. Barthes had long entertained the idea that photography could accomplish this by remaining stubbornly 'real' and refusing to be art (*Eiffel*, 71–3). In *Camera Lucida* 'the presence of a thing [in a photograph] . . . is never metaphoric' (*CL*, 78), and its 'certainty [of representation] is immediate' (*CL*, 115). As we have seen, Barthes argues that this realism is impossible in language – though he did sometimes argue that a sense of '*being there*' was possible in language, and with similar effects of 'astonishment' (*PoT*, 45–6). Barthes's conception of reality, therefore, as Naomi Schor has argued, is inevitably fragmentary because these moments are separate from the run of experience.[20] So what might a Barthesian realism look like?

Roland Barthes quotes Brecht to the effect that literature cannot cope with twentieth-century horrors like Auschwitz. 'Literature was not prepared for such events, and has not given itself the means to account for them' (*RB*, 119). The scale of modern atrocity 'explains our impotence to produce realistic literature' (*ibid.*):

> Realism is always timid, and there is too much *surprise* in a world which the mass media and the generalization of politics have made so profuse that it is no longer possible to figure it projectively: the world, as a literary object, escapes; knowledge deserts literature, which can no longer be either *Mimesis* [the imitation of reality] or *Mathesis* [a branch of learning] but merely *Semiosis*, the adventure of what is impossible to language, in a word *Text* . . . (*RB*, 119)

This is a familiar 'Textual' argument: the world is unrepresentable in language, so language is all there is. But this passage contains components for a different theory, and, as *Camera Lucida* makes clear, a new realism might turn on the idea of surprise, on the shock exerted on the literary itself.

As such it would develop the tradition of thought represented by the Russian Formalists, and connect with significant elements in contemporary practice. Brecht's remark was a contingent one, and Auschwitz has been represented, often by selecting a literary manner which jars with the subject matter. Primo Levi, an Auschwitz survivor, pits an unremittingly courageous humane rationalism, even comedy, against barbarity in his various works on his experience of the camps, and in Britain Geoffrey Hill's extraordinary poem 'September Song' plays the Holocaust against love songs, jazz classics, the sonnet, and an English pastoral garden in a breathtaking series of puns which mince the contemporary codes of representation and response.[21] Other recent writers also work with these effects: Kurt Vonnegut's novel *Slaughterhouse 5* (1969) dramatises Brecht's problem about appropriate language with reference to the Dresden fire-bombings; while Ciaran Carson's remarkable poems in *The Irish For No* (1987) play with different modes of narration and style against Dresden (again) and a range of colonial wars;[22] and so on. In turning back from the 'Text' towards the articulation of pain and elegy in *Camera Lucida*, Barthes is part of a powerfully contemporary structure of response in which the world is engaged through shock, surprise and the desire to rewrite the self caught in that drama.

The map of the self in *Camera Lucida* is very different from the psychology of depthlessness in recent postmodern revisions of traditional psychology.[23] In these theories the self is a surface on which images skate with fragmentary abandon. No particular image preserves the self's integrity, or locates it in a set of values or determinations. Late Barthes, however, works towards a more classically humanist pattern, stressing personal authenticity and a complex epistemological confidence. Individuals are 'weighed down' by images. The photographed individual thinks images are mere poses which reserve 'the precious essence of my individuality: what I am, apart from the effigy' (*CL*, 11–12). But 'it is the contrary that must be said: "myself" never coincides with my image; for it is the image which is heavy, motionless, stubborn (which is why society sustains it), and "myself" which is light, divided, dispersed' (*CL*, 12).

This is the oppressive condition endemic to sociality which has been Barthes's theme from the start, and the image here performs the role which in earlier work had been filled by 'Literature' or mythology. Indeed, Barthes reverts to earlier terminology: 'Alas, I am doomed by (well-meaning) Photography always to have an expression: my body never finds its zero degree' (*CL*, 12). But he adds a coda which is new: '(perhaps only my mother? For it is not indifference which erases the weight of the image – the Photomat always turns you into a criminal type, wanted by the police – but love, extreme love)' (*CL*, 12). Hitherto his reaction to the alienating bind of the social has been to run from 'Literature' or mythology into the zero degree or 'Textuality'. But Barthes now returns to the origins of the self, and to love.

Camera Lucida is dedicated 'In Homage to *L'Imaginaire* by Jean-Paul Sartre', and takes Barthes back to a very early theme: how is it possible to reconcile freedom with a social condition in which the self is pushed towards inauthenticity? *L'Imaginaire* (1940) argued that the imagination is existentially liberating. It is because we can imagine life to be otherwise that we have power over the world and ourselves. Whereas the standard stucturalist and poststructuralist argument had been that the imagination screens the individual from the real and accommodates him or her to the *status quo*, Sartre stresses that freedom is its very condition: 'it is because he is transcendentally free that man can imagine'.[24] By aligning himself with Sartre's early phenomenology, therefore, Barthes is once more reworking his earlier positions. He continues to portray the world as screened by illusion, but these illusions are now moveable.

The United States remained Barthes's example of a culture in which 'everything is transformed into images: only images exist and are produced and consumed' (*CL*, 118). But America is merely representative:

> What characterises the so-called advanced societies is that they today consume images and no longer, like those of the past, beliefs; they are therefore more liberal, less fanatical, but also more 'false' (less 'authentic') – something we translate, in ordinary consciousness, by the avowal of an impression of nauseated boredom, as if the universalized image were producing a world that is without difference (indifferent), from which can rise, here and there, only the cry of anarchisms, marginalisms, and individualisms: let us try to abolish the images, let us save immediate Desire (desire without mediation). (*CL*, 118–19)

We can see here the Barthesian dystopic scenario familiar from *Mythologies*, *The Fashion System* or *The Pleasure of the Text*: the world of nauseated boredom, of the insubstantial stereotype, of gullible passive consumption. But now there is a twist to this tale. If Barthes's poststructuralism juxtaposed the tight alternatives of conformist rationality or ecstatic release, *Camera Lucida* reformulates this opposition. In this passage there is a critique of representative positions of the 1960s such as those of the Situationists or Marcuse, who opposed the sterilities of the image to aboriginal, authentic desire. But the passage is also a form of self-criticism, for the 'ethical question' posed by the triumph of the image is that it 'completely de-realizes the human world of conflicts and desires' (*CL*, 118). In a sense this was always Barthes's theme, but here, arrestingly and in as many words, is an identifiable human world.

The concluding page of *Camera Lucida* once again formulates a binary alternative: 'Mad or tame? Photography can be one or the other.' Tame photography subjects 'its spectacle to the civilized code of perfect illusions'; mad photography confronts 'in it the wakening of intractable reality'. This final realism is 'absolute and, so to speak, original, obliging the loving and terrified consciousness to return to the very letter of Time' (*CL*, 119). Loving and terrified – in his finale Barthes remains the connoisseur of tragic oxymoron. The choice of 'mad' as an opposite of 'tame' is perhaps an unfortunate residue of schizo-analysis embalmed by bereavement, but this fugitive career which had fled 'Literature' and mythology into the 'Text' now confronts an 'intractable reality'. Alas, for Barthes and us, this was a last, grim word.

Notes

Historical and cultural context

1. Richard Howard, 'Remembering RB', in *Signs in Culture: Roland Barthes today*, ed. Steven Ungar and Betty R. McGraw (Iowa City, University of Iowa Press, 1989), pp. 32–6.

Chapter 1

1. Louis-Jean Calvet, *Roland Barthes 1915–1980* (Paris, Flammarion, 1990), pp. 80–3, 145.
2. Annette Lavers, *Roland Barthes: Structuralism and after* (London, Methuen, 1982), pp. 10, 52; Patrizia Lombardo, *The Three Paradoxes of Roland Barthes* (London, University of Georgia Press, 1989), p. 39.
3. Hayden White, *Metahistory: The historical imagination in nineteenth-century Europe* (London, Johns Hopkins University Press, 1973), *Tropics of Discourse* (London, Johns Hopkins University Press, 1978), and *The Content of the Form: Narrative discourse and historical representation* (London, Johns Hopkins University Press, 1987).
4. For accounts of the phenomenological school, see Sarah Lawall, *Critics of Consciousness: The existential structures of literature* (Cambridge, MA, Harvard University Press, 1968) and Frank Lentricchia, *After the New Criticism* (London, Methuen, 1983), ch. 3.
5. J. Hillis Miller, *Charles Dickens: The world of his novels* (London, Indiana University Press, 1969), p.ix. Subsequent page references will follow quotations.

6. John Carey, *The Violent Effigy: A study of Dickens's imagination* (London, Faber, 1979), pp. 9–10. Subsequent page references will follow quotations.
7. Doris Lessing, 'A small personal voice', in *Declaration*, ed. Tom Maschler (London, MacGibbon & Kee, 1957), pp. 11–28.
8. Sylvia Plath, *Collected Poems*, ed. Ted Hughes (London, Faber, 1981), p. 129.
9. Robert Graves, *The White Goddess: A historical grammar of poetic myth*, amended and enlarged edn (London, Faber, 1961), p. 14.
10. For instance, Jonathan Culler, *Barthes* (London, Fontana, 1983), pp. 43–5; Frances Bartkowski, 'Roland Barthes's secret garden', *Studies in Twentieth-Century Literature*, 5, 2 (1981), 133–46.
11. Calvet, *Barthes 1915–1980*, pp. 107–8.
12. Albert Camus, *Selected Essays and Notebooks*, ed. and trans. Philip Thody (Harmondsworth, Penguin, 1970), p. 222.
13. Thom Gunn, 'My life up to now', in *The Occasions of Poetry: Essays in criticism and autobiography*, ed. Clive Wilmer (London, Faber, 1982), p. 173.
14. Jean-Paul Sartre, *What is Literature?* trans. Bernard Frechtman (London, Methuen, 1967), p. 14.
15. Alain Robbe-Grillet, *For a New Novel: Essays on fiction*, trans. Richard Howard (New York, Grove Press, 1965). For Barthes's essays on Robbe-Grillet, see *Critical Essays*. Useful comment on the 'nouveau roman' may be found in Stephen Heath's *The Nouveau Roman: A study in the practice of writing* (London, Elek, 1972). Heath is one of Barthes's translators, and his account is a committed Barthesian one.
16. James Kelman, 'Interview with James Kelman', *Chapman*, 57 (1989), 1–9, and *Some Recent Attacks: Essays cultural and political* (Stirling, AK Press, 1992).
17. Wayne C. Booth, *Critical Understanding: The powers and limits of pluralism* (London, University of Chicago Press, 1979), p. 69.
18. For an excellent detailed discussion of Barthes's commentary on Racine, see Michael Moriarty, *Roland Barthes* (Cambridge, Polity, 1991), ch. 4.
19. Raymond Picard, *New Criticism or New Fraud?* trans. Frank Towne (np, Washington State University Press, 1969). All these words are used – usually more than once – in the course of the argument.
20. Serge Doubrovsky, *The New Criticism in France*, trans. Derek Coltman (London, University of Chicago Press, 1973), pp. 43–4. Subsequent page references will follow quotations.
21. Pierre Bourdieu, *Homo Academicus*, trans. Peter Collier (Cambridge, Polity, 1988), pp. xxii, 115–18. Barthes himself believed that the substance of the quarrel was largely territorial: Picard did not want Barthes trespassing on his academic 'game preserve' of Racine studies (*Grain*, 39–40).
22. Elizabeth W. Bruss, *Beautiful Theories: The spectacle of discourse in contemporary criticism* (London, Johns Hopkins University Press, 1982); Lentricchia, *After the New Criticism*.
23. Gerald Graff, *Literature Against Itself: Literary ideas in modern society* (London, University of Chicago Press, 1979).
24. 'The sapient structuralist', *Times Literary Supplement*, September 1964, p. 792.

25. 'Alien corn' and 'Island view', *Times Literary Supplement*, 6 August and 3 September 1964, pp. 695 and 803 respectively.
26. Philip Thody, *Roland Barthes: A conservative estimate* (London, Macmillan, 1977), p. 3.
27. Here and in what follows I am drawing on the following works which feature accounts of Barthes or his milieu, though for reasons of space, and following the lead of many of these books, I will not give specific reference: Lionel Abel, 'It isn't true and it doesn't rhyme', *Encounter*, 51 (1978), 33–57; John Bayley, 'The lost instructors', *Times Literary Supplement*, 12 February 1988, pp. 167–8; Denis Donoghue, *Ferocious Alphabets* (London, Faber, 1981); Graham Hough, 'Into a semiological wonderland', *Times Higher Education Supplement*, 21 April 1972, p. 15, and 'The importation of Roland Barthes', *Times Literary Supplement*, 9 December 1977, p. 1443; Leonard Jackson, *The Poverty of Structuralism: Literature and structuralist theory* (Harlow, Longmans, 1991); Gabriel Josipovici, *The World and the Book: A study of modern fiction* (London, Macmillan, 1971); Lawrence Lerner (ed.), *Reconstructing Literature* (Oxford, Basil Blackwell, 1983) – especially Lerner's introduction and the pieces by Roger Scruton and John Holloway; Patrick Parrinder, *The Failure of Theory: Essays on criticism and contemporary fiction* (Brighton, Harvester, 1987); Christopher Ricks, 'The adman's friend', *Sunday Times*, 5 March 1972, p. 35; Geoffrey Strickland, *Structuralism or Criticism? Thoughts on how we read* (Cambridge, Cambridge University Press, 1981); Philip Thody, *Roland Barthes* (see n.26); Peter Washington, *Fraud: Literary theory and the end of English* (London, Fontana, 1989).
28. Rick Rylance, *Psychological Theory and Victorian Culture 1850–1880* (Oxford, Clarendon Press, forthcoming).

Chapter 2

1. Bruss, *Beautiful Theories*, pp. 365–6.
2. Lavers, *Roland Barthes*, pp. 135, 175.
3. For example, Lavers, *ibid.*, Steven Ungar, *Roland Barthes: The professor of desire* (London, University of Nebraska Press, 1983), pp. 40–2; Eve Tavor Bannet, *Structuralism and the Logic of Dissent: Barthes, Derrida, Foucault, Lacan* (London, Macmillan, 1989), p. 4.
4. There are a number of more detailed guides to structuralist thought, virtually all of which give extended attention to Barthes's work: John Sturrock, *Structuralism* (London, Paladin, 1986) is a helpful general guide, while Fredric Jameson, *The Prison-House of Language* (London, Princeton University Press, 1972) and Terence Hawkes, *Structuralism and Semiotics* (London, Methuen, 1977) are useful for students of literature.
5. For a succinct guide, see Jonathan Culler, *Saussure* (London, Fontana, 1976), though Saussure's own *Course in General Linguistics*, trans. Wade Baskin (London, Fontana, 1974), or Roy Harris (London, Duckworth, 1983) is still the best place to start.

6. Louis-Jean Calvet, *Roland Barthes: un regard politique sur le signe* (Paris, Payart, 1973), p. 37.

7. There is no space to go into this here, but *The Fashion System* contains a compelling account (pp. 207–15) of how memory becomes committed to ruinous short duration by the endless oscillation of short-term syntagms in fashion and, by extension, all routinised semiotic systems.

8. For example, Gilbert Adair, *Myths and Memories* (London, Fontana, 1986) and Paul Rambali's entertaining and informative *French Blues: A not-so sentimental journey through lives and memories in modern France* (London, Heinemann, 1989). Len Masterson (ed.), *Television Mythologies: Stars, shows and signs* (London, Comedia, 1984) is a more conventional piece of criticism.

9. Calvet, *Barthes 1915–1980*, pp. 176–9.

10. Didier Eribon, *Michel Foucault*, trans. Betsy Wing (London, Faber, 1992), p. 294. See also Réda Bensmaïa, *The Barthes Effect: The essay as reflective text*, trans. Pat Fedkiew (Minneapolis, University of Minnesota Press, 1987).

11. Marshall McLuhan, *The Mechanical Bride: Folklore of industrial man* (London, Routledge & Kegan Paul, 1967), p. v.

12. Annie Cohen-Solal, *Sartre: A life* (London, Mandarin, 1991), pp. 363–4. For general information, see C.W.E. Bigsby (ed.), *Superculture: American popular culture and Europe* (Bowling Green, OH, Bowling Green Popular Press, 1975); Jacques Demarcq, *Les Années 50* (Paris, Éditions du Centre Pompidou, 1988); and Brian Rigby, *Popular Culture in Modern France: A study in cultural discourse* (London, Routledge, 1991).

13. Don McCullin (with Lewis Chester), *Unreasonable Behaviour: An autobiography* (London, Vintage, 1992), p. 35.

14. J.G. Merquior, *From Prague to Paris: A critique of structuralist and poststructuralist thought* (London, Verso, 1986).

15. For Althusser's version, see his famous essay 'Ideology and ideological state apparatuses' (1970), in *Essays on Ideology* (London, Verso, 1984), pp. 1–60. Both Althusser and Barthes found a significant source for these ideas in Lacan.

16. Iwana Blazwick (ed.), *Endless Passion . . . An Endless Banquet: The Situationist International from 1957 to 1962 and documents tracing the impact on British culture from the 1960s to the 1980s* (London, ICA/Verso, 1989).

17. Bannet, *Structuralism and the Logic of Dissent*, pp. 3–4; Thody, *Roland Barthes*, pp. 104–8. For overall discussion, see Keith Reader, *Intellectuals and the Left in France since 1968* (London, Macmillan, 1987).

18. Raymond Williams, 'Culture is ordinary', in *Resources of Hope: Culture, democracy, socialism*, ed. Robin Gable (London, Verso, 1989), p. 4. Subsequent page references will follow quotations.

19. For a more general discussion, see Michael Moriarty, 'The longest cultural journey: Raymond Williams and French theory', *Social Text*, 30 (1992), 57–77.

20. Quoted from Ragon's *Histoire de la littérature prolétarienne en France* (1973) by Lavers, *Roland Barthes*, p. 79.

21. Pierre Bourdieu, Preface to the English-language edition of *Distinction: A social critique of the judgements of taste*, trans. Richard Nice (London, Routledge & Kegan Paul, 1984), p. xi.

22. Jean-Claude Passeron, 'Introduction to *The Uses of Literacy*', trans. Richard Dyer, *Working Papers in Cultural Studies*, 1 (1971), 120–31.
23. Richard Hoggart, *The Uses of Literacy: Aspects of working-class life with special reference to publications and entertainments* (Harmondsworth, Penguin, 1958), pp. 171, 174, 178, 193, 248, 281. Subsequent page references will follow quotations.
24. See, in *Mythologies*, the essay on 'Toys', for instance, or the sub-Heideggerean claim in 'Myth today' that the alienation of language can be avoided if existence is powerfully in contact with work and action, as in the – suspiciously pastoral – world of the woodcutter (*Myth*, 145–6).
25. Andrew Ross, *No Respect: Intellectuals and popular culture* (London, Routledge, 1989), p. 211.
26. David Robbins (ed.), *The Independent Group: Postwar Britain and the aesthetics of plenty* (London, MIT Press, 1990).
27. John Berger, 'Mythical speech', *New Society*, 24 February 1972, pp. 407–8.
28. Angela Carter, 'Notes from the front line', in *On Gender and Writing*, ed. Michelene Wandor (London, Pandora, 1983), pp. 69–77.

Chapter 3

1. Paul de Man, 'The dead-end of formalist criticism' (1954), reprinted in *Blindness and Insight: Essays in the rhetoric of contemporary criticism*, trans. Wlad Godzich, 2nd edn (London, Methuen, 1983), pp. 229–45.
2. Paul de Man, 'Roland Barthes and the limits of structuralism', *Yale French Studies*, 77 (1990), 177–90.
3. Julia Kristeva, 'How does one speak to literature?' (1971) in *Desire in Language: A semiotic approach to literature and art*, ed. Leon S. Roudiez, trans. Thomas Gora, Alice Jardine and Leon S. Roudiez (Oxford, Basil Blackwell, 1981), pp. 92–123. Subsequent page references will follow quotations.
4. For accounts of *Tel Quel*, see Mary Ann Caws, '*Tel Quel*: text and revolution', *Diacritics*, 3 (1973), 2–8; Leslie Hill, 'Philippe Sollers and *Tel Quel*', in *Beyond the Nouveau Roman: Essays on the contemporary French novel*, ed. Michael Tilby (Oxford, Berg, 1990), pp. 100–22; and Charles Russell, *Poets, Prophets and Revolutionaries: The literary avant-garde from Rimbaud through postmodernism* (Oxford, Oxford University Press, 1985).
5. For Barthes's debt to Kristeva, see 'Kristeva's *Semeiotike*' (1970) (*Rustle*, 168–71) and, especially, 'Theory of the text' (1973). For comment, see Lavers, *Roland Barthes*, pp. 170–5.
6. George P. Landow, *Hypertext: The convergence of contemporary critical theory and technology* (London, Johns Hopkins University Press, 1992), p. 3.
7. For further comment on this aspect of Barthes's work, see Ungar, *The Professor of Desire*, ch. 5.
8. For discussion of these matters, see Mary Bittner Wiseman, *The Ecstasies of Roland Barthes* (London, Routledge, 1989), especially chs. 4 and 5. See also Lavers, *Roland Barthes*, pp. 204 ff. for useful contextual comment.
9. Lombardo, *Three Paradoxes*, pp. 64–5.

10. Michael Riffaterre, 'Sade, or text as fantasy', *Diacritics*, 2 (1972), 3.
11. Frank Kermode, 'The use of codes', in *Approaches to Poetics: Selected papers from the English Institute*, ed. Seymour Chatman (London, Columbia University Press, 1973), pp. 51–79, and the 'Prologue' to *Essays on Fiction 1971–82* (London, Routledge & Kegan Paul, 1983).
12. Jerome J. McGann, 'The text, the poem, and the problem of historical method', in *The Beauty of Inflections: Literary investigations in historical method and theory* (Oxford, Clarendon Press, 1985). Fredric Jameson has an interesting discussion of the same problem in 'Pleasure: a political issue' in *The Ideologies of Theory: Essays 1971–86* (London, Routledge, 1988), vol. 2.
13. Barbara Johnson, 'The critical difference: BartheS/BalZac', in *The Critical Difference: Essays in the contemporary rhetoric of reading* (London, Johns Hopkins University Press, 1980), pp. 3–12.
14. For a succinct overview, see William Ray, *Literary Meaning: From phenomenology to deconstruction* (Oxford, Basil Blackwell, 1984).
15. Lavers, *Roland Barthes*, p. 205; Bourdieu, *Distinction*, pp. 498–500.
16. Richard Rorty, 'Nineteenth-century idealism and twentieth-century textualism', in *Consequences of Pragmatism (Essays: 1972–1980)* (Brighton, Harvester, 1982), pp. 139–59.
17. Philippe Sollers, 'The novel and the experience of limits', in *Writing and the Experience of Limits*, trans. Philip Barnard with David Hayman (New York, Columbia University Press, 1983), p. 188.
18. Sollers, 'Reading *S/Z*', in *Signs of the Times: Introductory readings in textual semiotics*, eds Stephen Heath, Colin MacCabe and Christopher Prendergast (Cambridge, np, 1971), p. 38.
19. Jacques Derrida, *Of Grammatology*, trans. Gayatri Chakravorty Spivak (London, Johns Hopkins University Press, 1976), pp. 332–3.
20. Marshall McLuhan, *The Guttenberg Galaxy: The making of typographic man* (London, Routledge & Kegan Paul, 1962), p. 278.
21. Marshall McLuhan, *Understanding Media: The extensions of man* (London, Sphere, 1964; 1967 (pbk)), p.11. Subsequent page references will follow quotations.
22. Herbert Marcuse, *An Essay on Liberation* (Harmondsworth, Penguin, 1969), p. 44.
23. Jonathon Green (ed.), *Days in the Life: Voices from the English underground 1961–1971* (London, Heinemann, 1988), pp. 11, 62–3, 246.
24. Jameson, 'Periodizing the 60s', in *The Ideologies of Theory*, vol. 2, pp. 178–208.
25. Jonathan Miller, *McLuhan* (New York, Viking, 1971).
26. Jameson, 'Pleasure: a political issue', p. 63.
27. N. Katherine Hayles, 'Information or noise? Economy of explanation in Barthes's *S/Z* and Shannon's information theory', in *One Culture: Essays in science and literature*, ed. George Levine (London, University of Wisconsin Press, 1987), p. 127. Subsequent page references will follow quotations. See also Mary McGhee Wood, 'Signification and simulation: Barthes's response to Turing', *Paragraph*, 11 (1983), 210–26.
28. Philippe Sollers, from *Paradis*, trans. Carl Lovitt in *In the Wake of the Wake*, ed. David Hayman and Elliott Anderson (Madison, University of Wisconsin Press, 1978), p. 101. Compare Barthes in 'To the seminar' (1974), where he

argues, in a postmodern manner, that culture is necessary not 'as a direct value but as an invented one: Kitsch, plagiarism, game, pleasure, shimmer of parody language *in which we believe* and *we do not believe* (the characteristic of farce), a fragment of pastiche . . . ' (*Rustle*, 342).

29. Howard Barker, 'The small discovery of dignity', in *New Theatre Voices of the Seventies*, ed. Simon Trussler (London, Methuen, 1981), pp. 195, 187, 193.

30. Howard Barker, '49 asides for a tragic theatre', *The Guardian*, 10 February 1986, p. 11.

31. Howard Barker, *ibid.*, 'The triumph in defeat', *The Guardian*, 22 August 1988, p. 34; 'Understanding exits as complexity takes a bow', *Times Higher Education Supplement*, 5 January 1990, p. 16. Subsequent references will be noted in the text. I have developed some of these arguments further in 'Forms of dissent in contemporary drama and contemporary theatre', in *The Death of the Playwright? Modern British drama and literary theory*, ed. Adrian Page (London, Macmillan 1992), pp. 115–41.

32. Howard Barker, *The Last Supper: A New Testament* (London, John Calder, 1988). The programme-text contained interleaved, unnumbered pages, from which this quotation is taken.

Chapter 4

1. I.A. Richards, *Principles of Literary Criticism*, 2nd edn (London, Routledge, 1960), p. 105.

2. James Joyce, *A Portrait of the Artist as a Young Man*, ed. J.S. Atherton (London, Heinemann, 1964), p. 75

3. Maud Ellmann, 'Dismembering Dedalus: "A Portrait of the Artist as a Young Man"', in *Untying the Text: A poststructuralist reader*, ed. Robert Young (London, Routledge & Kegan Paul, 1981), pp. 189–206.

4. Quoted in Bensmaïa, *The Barthes Effect*, p. 24.

5. Gilles Deleuze and Félix Guattari, *Anti-Oedipus: Capitalism and schizophrenia*, trans. Robert Hurley, Mark Seem and Helen R. Lane (New York, Viking, 1977). For contextual comment, see Sherry Turkle, *Psychoanalytic Politics: Freud's French Revolution* (London, Burnett Books, 1979), ch. 6.

6. For a succinct overview, see Robert Hewison, *Too Much: Art and society in the sixties 1960–75* (London, Methuen, 1986), chs 3, 5.

7. R.D. Laing, *The Divided Self: An existential study in sanity and madness* (London, Tavistock, 1960), p. 17.

8. Jacques Lacan, *Écrits: A selection*, trans. Alan Sheridan (London, Tavistock, 1977), p. 2.

9. Émile Benveniste, *Problems in General Linguistics*, trans. Mary Elizabeth Meek (Coral Gables, University of Miami Press, 1971).

10. In both *Roland Barthes* and *A Lover's Discourse*, Barthes writes interestingly about the idea of influence in monetary terms: influences are borrowed (*RB*, 74), or 'levied on the intellectual culture of the moment' (*RB*, 99). In *A Lover's Discourse*, which is a mosaic of references and allusions, the author

'lends his "culture" to the amorous subject' (*LD*, 9) to situate the discourse in a more open cultural field.

11. Leslie Hill, 'Barthes's body', *Paragraph*, 11 (1988), 107–26; Ann Jefferson, 'Bodymatters: self and others in Bakhtin, Sartre and Barthes', in *Bakhtin and Cultural Theory*, ed. Ken Hirschkop and David Shepherd (Manchester, Manchester University Press, 1989), pp. 152–77.
12. Culler, *Barthes*, ch. 10.
13. Rick Rylance, 'Lawrence's politics', in *Rethinking Lawrence*, ed. Keith Brown (Milton Keynes, Open University Press, 1990), pp. 163–80.
14. Moriarty, *Roland Barthes*, p. 188.
15. This idea is explored further in Wiseman, *The Ecstasies of Roland Barthes*, ch. 6.
16. Angela Carter, *The Magic Toyshop* (London, Virago, 1981), p. 1.
17. John Haffenden (ed.), *Novelists in Interview* (London, Methuen, 1985), p. 80.
18. Edward W. Said, *Orientalism* (London, Routledge & Kegan Paul, 1978). See also Lisa Lowe, *Critical Terrains: French and British orientalisms* (London, Cornell University Press, 1992); Lynn A. Higgins, 'Barthes's imaginary voyages', *Studies in Twentieth-Century Literature*, 5 (1981), 157–74; and Diana Knight, 'Roland Barthes in harmony: the writing of utopia', *Paragraph*, 11 (1988), 127–42.
19. Lavers, *Roland Barthes*, p. 214; Moriarty, *Roland Barthes*, p. 198. See also Ungar, *Roland Barthes: The professor of desire*, ch. 8.
20. Naomi Schor, 'Desublimation: Roland Barthes's aesthetics', in *Reading in Detail: Aesthetics and the feminine* (London, Methuen, 1987), pp. 79–97.
21. Geoffrey Hill, *Collected Poems* (Harmondsworth, Penguin, 1985), p. 67.
22. Ciaran Carson, *The Irish For No* (Dublin, The Gallery Press/Winston-Salem, Wake Forest University Press, 1987).
23. Moriarty, *Roland Barthes*, p. 207.
24. Jean-Paul Sartre, *The Psychology of the Imagination* (English translation of *L'Imaginaire*), translator unacknowledged (London, Methuen, 1972), p. 216.

Select bibliography

Works by Barthes

Camera Lucida: Reflections on Photography, trans. Richard Howard (London, Fontana, 1984); *La Chambre claire: note sur la photographie* (Paris, Gallimard/Seuil, 1980)

Critical Essays, trans. Richard Howard (Evanston, IL, Northwestern University Press, 1972); *Essais critiques*, 2nd edn (Paris, Seuil, 1971)

Criticism and Truth, trans. Katrine Pilcher Keuneman (London, Athlone Press, 1987); *Critique et vérité* (Paris, Seuil, 1966)

The Eiffel Tower and Other Mythologies, trans. Richard Howard (New York, Hill & Wang, 1979); (see *Mythologies* below for details of the French edition)

Elements of Semiology (see *Writing Degree Zero* below)

Empire of Signs, trans. Richard Howard (London, Jonathan Cape, 1983); *L'empire des signes* (Geneva, Skira, 1970)

The Fashion System, trans. Matthew Ward and Richard Howard (London, Jonathan Cape, 1985); *Système de la mode* (Paris, Seuil, 1967)

The Grain of the Voice: Interviews 1962–1980, trans. Linda Coverdale (London, Jonathan Cape, 1981); *Le Grain de la voix: entretiens 1962–1980* (Paris, Seuil, 1981)

Image-Music-Text, essays selected and trans. Stephen Heath (London, Fontana, 1977)

Incidents, trans. Richard Howard (Oxford, University of California Press, 1992); *Incidents* (Paris, Seuil, 1987)

A Lover's Discourse: Fragments, trans. Richard Howard (London, Jonathan Cape, 1979); *Fragments d'un discours amoureux* (Paris, Seuil, 1977)

Michelet, trans. Richard Howard (New York, Hill & Wang, 1987); *Michelet par lui-même* (Paris, Seuil, 1954)

Mythologies, selected and trans. Annette Lavers (London, Granada, 1973); *Mythologies* (Paris, Seuil, 1957). (See also *The Eiffel Tower*.)

New Critical Essays, trans. Richard Howard (New York, Hill & Wang 1980); *Nouveaux essais critiques* (published with *Le Degré zéro de l'écriture*, Paris, Seuil, 1972)

On Racine, trans. Richard Howard (New York, Octagon Books, 1977); *Sur Racine* (Paris, Seuil, 1963)

The Pleasure of the Text, trans. Richard Miller (New York, Hill & Wang 1975); *Le Plaisir du texte* (Paris, Seuil, 1973)

The Responsibilities of Forms: Critical essays on music, art and representation, trans. Richard Howard (Oxford, Basil Blackwell, 1986); *L'Obvie et l'obtus: essais critiques III* (Paris, Seuil, 1982)

Roland Barthes by Roland Barthes, trans. Richard Howard (London, Macmillan, 1977); *Roland Barthes par Roland Barthes* (Paris, Seuil, 1975)

The Rustle of Language, trans. Richard Howard (Oxford, Basil Blackwell, 1986); *Le Bruissement de la langue: essais critiques IV* (Paris, Seuil, 1984)

Sade/Fourier/Loyola, trans. Richard Miller (New York, Hill & Wang, 1977); *Sade/Fourier/Loyola* (Paris, Seuil, 1971)

Selected Writings, ed. Susan Sontag (London, Fontana, 1983)

The Semiotic Challenge, trans. Richard Howard (Oxford, Basil Blackwell, 1988); *L'Aventure sémiologique* (Paris, Seuil, 1985)

Sollers Writer, trans. Philip Thody (London, Athlone Press, 1984); *Sollers écrivain* (Paris, Seuil, 1979)

S/Z, trans. Richard Miller (New York, Hill & Wang, 1974); *S/Z* (Paris, Seuil, 1970)

'Theory of the text', trans. Ian McLeod, in *Untying the Text: A Poststructuralist Reader*, ed. Robert Young (London, Routledge & Kegan Paul, 1981), pp. 31–47

Writing Degree Zero and Elements of Semiology, trans. Annette Lavers and Colin Smith (Boston, MA, Beacon Press, 1970); *Le Degré zéro de l'écriture et Éléments de sémiologie* (Paris, Denoël/Gonthier, 1965)

Secondary works

Biography

Calvet, Louis-Jean, *Roland Barthes, 1915–1980* (Paris, Flammarion, 1990)

Books on Barthes

Calvet, Louis-Jean, *Roland Barthes: un regard politique sur le signe* Paris, Payart, 1973) [useful mid-career survey]

Culler, Jonathan, *Barthes* (London, Fontana, 1983) [a succinct introduction]

Heath, Stephen, *Vertige du déplacement: lecture de Barthes* (Paris, Fayard, 1974) [valuable mid-career assessment]

Lavers, Annette, *Roland Barthes: Structuralism and after* (London, Methuen, 1982) [especially good on the earlier career]

Lombardo, Patrizia, *The Three Paradoxes of Roland Barthes* (London, University of Georgia Press, 1989) [traces the paradox of Barthes's traditionalist radicalism]

Moriarty, Michael, *Roland Barthes* (Cambridge, Polity, 1991) [the best overall discussion]

Roger, Philippe, *Roland Barthes, Roman* (Paris, Grasset, 1986) [a lively account of the leading issues in Barthes's work]

Thody, Philip, *Roland Barthes: A conservative estimate* (London, Macmillan, 1977) [some useful detail]

Unger, Steven, *Roland Barthes: The professor of desire* (London, University of Nebraska Press, 1983) [useful on Barthes's poststructuralism]

Ungar, Steven and McGraw, Betty R. (eds), *Signs in Culture: Roland Barthes today* (Iowa City, University of Iowa Press, 1989) [a collection of essays of uneven interest]

Wasserman, George R., *Roland Barthes* (Boston, MA, Twayne, 1981) [lucid, if rather simplified, overview]

Wiseman, Mary Bittner, *The Ecstasies of Roland Barthes* (London, Routledge, 1989) [intelligent series of 'personal responses' to Barthes in a poststructuralist idiom]

Barthes in context

These books contain illuminating commentary on Barthes's work as part of a wider discussion.

Bannet, Eve Tavor, *Structuralism and the Logic of Dissent: Barthes, Derrida, Foucault, Lacan* (London, Macmillan, 1989)

Bruss, Elizabeth W., *Beautiful Theories: The spectacle of discourse in contemporary criticism* (London, Johns Hopkins University Press, 1982)

Coward, Rosalind and Ellis, John, *The Language of Materialism: Developments in semiology and the theory of the subject* (London, Routledge and Kegan Paul, 1977)

Culler, Jonathan, *Structuralist Poetics: Structuralism, linguistics and the study of literature* (London, Routledge & Kegan Paul, 1975)

Hawkes, Terence, *Structuralism and Semiotics* (London, Methuen, 1977)

Heath, Stephen, *The Nouveau Roman: A study in the practice of writing* (London, Elek, 1972)

Jameson, Fredric, *The Prison-House of Language: A critical account of structuralism and Russian formalism* (London, Princeton University Press, 1972)

Jameson, Fredric, *The Ideologies of Theory: Essays 1971–86*, 2 vols (London, Routledge, 1988)

Landow, George P., *Hypertext: The convergence of contemporary critical theory and technology* (London, Johns Hopkins University Press, 1992)

Merquior, J.G., *From Prague to Paris: A critique of structuralist and poststructuralist thought* (London, Verso, 1986)

Rambali, Paul, *French Blues: A journey through modern France* (London, Heinemann, 1989)

Ray, William, *Literary Meaning: From phenomenology to deconstruction* (Oxford, Basil Blackwell, 1984)

Reader, Keith A., *Intellectuals and the Left in France since 1968* (London, Macmillan, 1987)

Rorty, Richard, *Consequences of Pragmatism (Essays: 1972–1980)* (Brighton, Harvester, 1982)

Sturrock, John, *Structuralism* (London, Paladin, 1986)

Todorov, Tzvetan, *Literature and Its Theorists: A personal view of twentieth-century criticism*, trans. Catherine Porter (London, Routledge & Kegan Paul, 1988)

Contextual materials

The following offer useful opportunities for comparison with Barthes's work. Many are discussed in the course of this book.

Althusser, Louis, *Essays on Ideology* (London, Verso, 1984)

Benveniste, Émile, *Problems in General Linguistics*, trans. Mary Elizabeth Meek (Coral Gables, University of Miami Press, 1971)

Berger, John, *Ways of Seeing* (Harmondsworth, Penguin/BBC, 1972)

Brecht, Bertolt, *Brecht on Theatre*, ed. and trans. John Willett (London, Methuen, 1978)

Carter, Angela, *The Magic Toyshop* (London, Virago, 1981)

Carter, Angela, *Nothing Sacred: Selected writings* (London, Virago, 1982)

Debord, Guy, *The Society of the Spectacle* (np, Rebel Press/Aim Publications, 1987)

Deleuze, Gilles and Guattari, Félix, *Anti-Oedipus: Capitalism and schizophrenia*, trans. Robert Hurley, Mark Seem and Helen R. Lane (New York, Viking, 1977)

Derrida, Jacques, *Of Grammatology*, trans. Gayatri Chakravorty Spivak (London, Johns Hopkins University Press, 1976)

Derrida, Jacques, *Writing and Difference*, trans. Alan Bass (London, Routledge & Kegan Paul, 1978)

Foucault, Michel, *Madness and Civilisation: A history of insanity in the age of reason*, abridged and translated by Richard Howard (New York, Pantheon, 1965)

Foucault, Michel, *The Order of Things: An archeology of the human sciences*, translator unacknowledged (New York, Vintage Books, 1970)

Foucault, Michel, *The Foucault Reader*, ed. Paul Rabinow (Harmondsworth, Penguin, 1986)

Hoggart, Richard, *The Uses of Literacy: Aspects of working-class life with special reference to publications and entertainments* (Harmondsworth, Penguin, 1958)

Kristeva, Julia, *Desire in Language: A semiotic approach to literature and art*, ed. Leon S. Roudiez, trans. Thomas Gora, Alice Jardine and Leon S. Roudiez (Oxford, Basil Blackwell, 1982)

Kristeva, Julia, *The Kristeva Reader*, ed. Toril Moi (Oxford, Basil Blackwell, 1986)

Lacan, Jacques, *Écrits: A selection*, trans. Alan Sheridan (London, Tavistock, 1977)

Laing, R.D., *The Divided Self: An existential study of sanity and madness* (London, Tavistock, 1960)

McLuhan, Marshall, *The Guttenberg Galaxy: The making of typographic man* (London, Routledge & Kegan Paul, 1962)

McLuhan, Marshall, *Understanding Media: The extensions of man* (London, Sphere, 1964; 1967 (pbk))

McLuhan, Marshall, *The Mechanical Bride: Folklore of industrial man* (London, Routledge & Kegan Paul, 1967) (Originally published 1951)

Marcuse, Herbert, *An Essay on Liberation* (Harmondsworth, Penguin, 1969)

Neville, Richard, *Play Power*, (London, Jonathan Cape, 1970)

Robbe-Grillet, Alain, *For a New Novel: Essays on fiction*, trans. Richard Howard (New York, Grove Press, 1965)

Sartre, Jean-Paul, *What is Literature?* trans. Bernard Frechtman (London, Methuen, 1967)

Sartre, Jean-Paul, *The Psychology of the Imagination*, translator unacknowledged (London, Methuen, 1972)

Sollers, Philippe, *Writing and the Experience of Limits*, trans. Philip Barnard with David Hayman (New York, Columbia University Press, 1983)

Williams, Raymond, *The Long Revolution* (London, Chatto & Windus, 1961)

Williams, Raymond, *Resources of Hope: Culture, democracy, socialism*, ed. Robin Gable (London, Verso, 1989)

Studies of aspects of Barthes's work

In most cases the topic tackled is clear from the title. More specific reference is included where necessary.

Bartowski, Frances, 'Roland Barthes's secret garden', *Studies in Twentieth-Century Literature*, 5, 2 (1981), 133–46 [on Barthes and the body]

Bensmaïa, Réda, *The Barthes Effect: The essay as reflective text*, trans. Pat Fedkiew (Minneapolis, University of Minnesota Press, 1987)

Bourdieu, Pierre, *Distinction: A social critique of the judgement of taste*, trans. Richard Nice (London, Routledge & Kegan Paul, 1984)

Bourdieu, Pierre, *Homo Academicus*, trans. Peter Collier (Cambridge, Polity, 1988)

Champagne, Roland, *Literary History in the Wake of Roland Barthes: Redefining the myths of reading* (Birmingham, AL, Summa Publications, 1984)

de Man, Paul, 'The dead-end of formalist criticism' in *Blindness and Insight: Essays in the rhetoric of contemporary criticism*, 2nd edn, trans. Wlad Godzich (London, Methuen, 1983) pp. 229–45

de Man, Paul, 'Roland Barthes and the limits of structuralism', *Yale French Studies*, 77 (1990), 177–90

Doubrovsky, Serge, *The New Criticism in France*, trans. Derek Coltman (London, University of Chicago Press, 1973)

Easthope, Antony, *British Poststructuralism Since 1968* (London, Routledge, 1988)

Goodheart, Eugene, *The Skeptic Disposition in Contemporary Criticism* (Guildford, NJ, Princeton University Press, 1984)

Graff, Gerald, *Literature Against Itself: Literary ideas in modern society* (London, University of Chicago Press, 1979)

Hayles, N. Katherine, 'Information or noise? Economy of explanation in Barthes's *S/Z* and Shannon's information theory', in *One Culture: Essays in science and literature*, ed. George Levine (London, University of Wisconsin Press, 1987), pp. 119–42

Heath, Stephen, 'Barthes on love', *SubStance*, 37/38 (1983), 100–6

Higgins, Lynn A., 'Barthes's imaginary voyages', *Studies in Twentieth-Century Literature*, 5 (1981), 157–74

Hill, Leslie, 'Barthes's body', *Paragraph*, 11 (1988), 107–26

Jefferson, Ann, 'Bodymatters: self and others in Bakhtin, Sartre and Barthes', in *Bakhtin and Cultural Theory*, ed. Ken Hirschkop and David Shepherd (Manchester, Manchester University Press, 1989), pp. 152–77

Jefferson, Ann, 'Autobiography as intertext: Barthes, Saurraute, Robbe-Grillet', in *Intertextuality: Theories and practices* (Manchester, Manchester University Press, 1990), pp. 108–29

Johnson, Barbara, 'The critical difference: BartheS/BalZac' in *The Critical Difference: Essays in the contemporary rhetoric of criticism* (London, Johns Hopkins University Press, 1980)

Josipovici, Gabriel, *The World and the Book: A study of modern fiction* (London, Macmillan, 1971), ch. 11 [a discussion of the Barthes–Picard quarrel]

Kermode, Frank, 'The use of codes', in *Approaches to Poetics: Selected papers from the English Institute* (London, Columbia University Press, 1973), pp. 51–79

Knight, Diana, 'Roland Barthes in harmony: the writing of utopia', *Paragraph*, 11 (1988), 127–42

Knight, Diana, 'Roland Barthes: an intertextual figure', in *Intertextuality: Theories and practices* (Manchester, Manchester University Press, 1990), pp. 92–107

Knight, Diana, 'Roland Barthes: structuralism utopian and scientific', *News From Nowhere*, 9 (1991), 18–28

Lipking, Lawrence, 'Life, death and other theories', in *Historical Studies and Literary Criticism*, ed. Jerome J. McGann (Madison, University of Wisconsin Press, 1985), pp. 180–95 [an attack on Barthes's theory of 'the death of the author']

MacCabe, Colin, 'Class of '68: elements of an intellectual autobiography 1967–81', in *Theoretical Essays: Film, linguistics, literature* (Manchester, Manchester University Press, 1985), pp. 1–32

McGann, Jerome J., 'The text, the poem and the problem of historical method', in *The Beauty of Inflections: Literary investigations in historical method and theory* (Oxford, Clarendon Press, 1985)

Norris, Christopher, 'Roland Barthes: the view from here', *Critical Quarterly*, 20 (1978), 27–43

O'Donovan, Patrick, 'The place of rhetoric', *Paragraph*, 11 (1988), 227–48

Picard, Raymond, *New Criticism or New Fraud?* trans. Frank Towne (np, Washington State University Press, 1969)

Riffaterre, Michael, 'Sade, or text as fantasy', *Diacritics*, 2 (1972), 2–9

Runyan, Randolph, *Fowles/Irving/Barthes: Canonical variations on an apocryphal theme* (Miami, Ohio State University Press, 1981)

Russell, Charles, *Poets, Prophets and Revolutionaries: The literary avant-garde from Rimbaud through postmodernism* (Oxford, Oxford University Press, 1985)

Said, Edward W., 'Overcoming the thereness of things', *New York Times Book Review*, 30 July 1972, pp. 5, 15, [on *Mythologies*].

Said, Edward W., *Beginnings: Intention and method* (New York, Basic Books, 1975)

Said, Edward W., 'Opponents, audiences, constituencies, and community', in *The Politics of Interpretation*, ed. W.J.T. Mitchell (London, University of Chicago Press, 1983), pp. 7–32

Schor, Naomi, 'Desublimation: Roland Barthes's aesthetics', in *Reading in Detail: Aesthetics and the feminine* (London, Methuen, 1987), pp. 79–97

Schor, Naomi, 'Dreaming dissymmetry: Barthes, Foucault and sexual difference', in *Men in Feminism*, ed. Alice Jardine and Paul Smith (London, Methuen, 1987), pp. 98–110

Smyth, John Vignaux, *A Question of Eros: Irony in Sterne, Kierkegaard and Barthes* (Tallahassee, Florida State University Press, 1986)

Sturrock, John, 'Roland Barthes', in *Structuralism and Since* (Oxford, Oxford University Press, 1979), pp. 52–82

Thomas, Jean-Jacques, 'Sensationalism', *Studies in Twentieth-Century Literature*, 5 (1981), 205–17 [on Barthes's style]

Ulmer, Gregory L., 'The discourse of the imaginary', *Diacritics*, 10 (1980), 61–75

Wood, Mary McGhee, 'Signification and simulation: Barthes's response to Turing', *Paragraph*, 11 (1983), 210–26

Wood, Nigel, 'Contextualizing "Ecriture": Barthes and Foucault on simplicity' in *Cross-References: Modern French theory and the practice of criticism*, ed. David Kelley and Isabelle Clasera (London, Society for French Studies, 1986), pp. 148–59

Index